KATHLEEN SHERMAN

SHAMANIC MEDICAL INTUITIVE

YOU'RE NOT
CRAZY,

You're Simply a Psychic Medium

A GUIDE TO AWAKEN YOUR DIVINE PSYCHIC ABILITIES

You're Not Crazy, You're Simply a Psychic Medium!
A Guidebook to Awaken Your Divine Psychic Abilities

ISBN: 979-8-9855155-4-1

Cover design by: Keith Tarrier @ www.keithtarrier.com
Book design and layout by: Keith Tarrier
Editing by: Angela Haworth @ www.jotzycreatives.com

Dedication

I dedicate this book to all of my wonderful mentors, teachers, family and friends who have helped me blossom, grow and find my way on my spiritual journey. To my husband, and love of my life, Tim, who has always been my rock, my partner, and my confidant. To my two amazing daughters, Sierra and Lexie. Thank you for choosing me to be your mother, as that has been my greatest accomplishment, and purpose of my life! You bring me so much joy and happiness. I love you so much! Kathleen

Introducing Kathleen and Her Books

I am honored to join you on your spiritual journey! This is the second book that I have channeled with my loving team of light guiding me to assist you on your path to open to your true divine nature, help you become more intuitive, balance your energy, and live your life with more peace and harmony.

My first book, You're Not Crazy, You're Simply Divine, A Guide to Help You Step into Your Soul's True Purpose, shares my personal experiences of my wild and unexpected spiritual awakening and some of these experiences can be anticipated for your spiritual awakening. This book is a wonderful place to begin your spiritual journey of knowledge and it explains how to get through spiritual experiences that you may not understand. It was written to help those who feel lost and for those who want to gain a better understanding of the world of the unknown. It is a book that I wished I had when I went through my experience because it contains the foundational knowledge that will help you as you start on your journey of awakening.

In this series, the second book titled You're Not Crazy, You're Simply A Psychic Medium, A Guidebook to Awaken Your Divine Psychic Abilities, is a more advanced and comprehensive guide for learning advanced techniques for your psychic and mediumship abilities. This book deep dives into the psyche, spiritual dimensions, intuition, Akashic records, advanced mediumship techniques, and much more. It will help you go much deeper into your spiritual practice, connect with greater meaning with your spiritual helpers, and will help you to learn who they are and how they can assist you in your life.

I thank my entire spiritual team of light and all my beautiful friends and family that have enriched my life and have helped me on my path! This helped me to spiritually awaken and step into my spiritual gifts as a psychic medium, natural shaman, medical intuitive, and healer, and has helped me to become the oracle I was born to be. I now gift my knowledge forward to you to help break down the blocks that keep you from that important sacred knowledge. Many people and Spirit call these mystery teachings or mystery schools. Many of the ancient civilizations knew of this esoteric knowledge, and that is what it is meant to do, to help you open what has been buried for thousands of years.

My team of light wants you to know that you are divinely guided and that is why you are here! Take whatever resonates with you and let your Guides teach you in your own style! Don't get stuck on what you've been taught in the past. It's time to break down the old ways of the past. It's time for a new world! You and many others are paving the new path and way of the future to a more connected and happier future of living in Divine alignment. Keep following your instincts. If it feels right, then FOLLOW THAT PATH. You are on a new journey that is filled with lessons and new awakenings, all of which will lead you to a better way of life that you could only imagine in your wildest dreams.

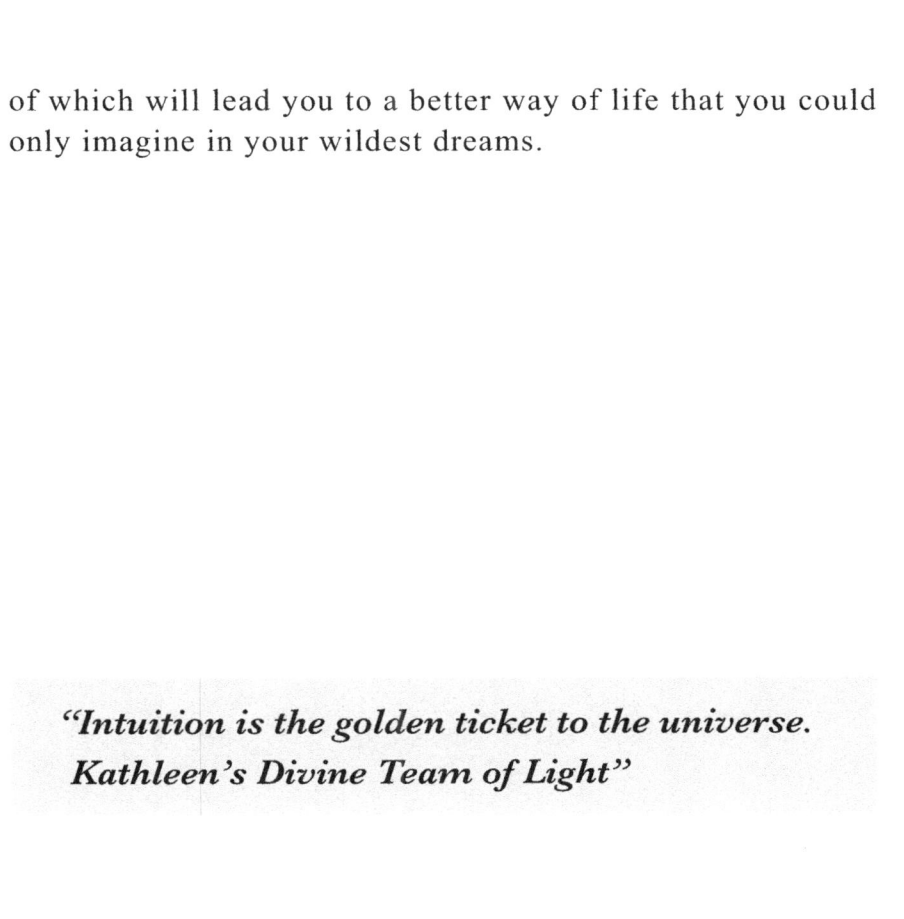

"Intuition is the golden ticket to the universe. Kathleen's Divine Team of Light"

Table of Contents

Chapter 1

OPENING THE DOOR TO THE WORLD OF THE DIVINE!

Chapter 1

Opening the Door to the World of the Divine!

Have you ever wondered how psychics and mediums talk to the deceased? I used to wonder the same thing until I had a wild and unexpected spiritual awakening. After my mother's death from this Earthly dimension in 2014, she spoke to me while on a run in the country. This experience was life-changing and eye-opening. The 3D existence I knew growing up and lived in had just expanded and shattered my old belief system. Before this experience, I had no clue that I had any type of psychic abilities. This was my ticket to a new way of living. I went on a journey of spiritual self-exploration to become an intuitive reader, healer, and teacher for others on the spiritual path of expansion. I am writing this book to help you open to your God-given spiritual gifts of psychic intuition, mediumship abilities, and inner knowing.

My question to each reader is, why. WHY are you interested in the great mysteries of the world? What is driving your curiosity to learn more? Since the beginning of time, there have been many who were seeking those answers. Our ancestors on Earth had many experiences of enlightened lifetimes. Maybe you have some sort of sense that you have lived in another time and place doing something extraordinary. Have you had visions or dreams in another time and place? You may also have a deep sense of knowing that you had a lifetime in a specific place because it feels like home.

Those memories are breaking through the veils of amnesia that you were born with. They are little snippets from the Divine helping you realize that you are much more than the human that has always been living a normal and routine life. They are windows into your soul, waiting to reveal themselves like an exciting adventure series. There is so much more to human existence than we know of, and we are all just beginning on that amazing ride of deep exploration into the world of the unknown. If you allow yourself to open up to these amazing experiences, it will help you shift your life. You may be working a job you despise, or be in a toxic relationship, or you may be physically or emotionally ill or unhappy. Something is pushing up from below that needs to be cleansed and healed. When you learn to bring this up to the surface and face it head-on, you can release, cleanse, heal, and move forward. Those pieces of shadows within yourself are the results of trauma from past and current lifetimes. By facing these shadows and working your way through them with grace, you help your soul to heal and shine brighter. The purpose of all of this is to release what is not working in your life and to help you find the courage to make a change. It will help each of you to realize the areas where you are living your life in fear, denial, and victimhood. Each one of us must face our fears so that we may be our own savior.

We, as humans, are evolving as a species to higher and higher levels of consciousness, which means we are spiritually awakening in waves of groups. As the consciousness levels rise, our shadows surface to be healed. After you face these shadows and heal from them, you will rise to the next level. This allows us to be more intuitive, sensing things that weren't visible before. In a nutshell, we are becoming more psychic, sensitive, and intuitive beings. We can feel the emotions and feelings of other humans and animals. This helps you to be a more compassionate human and tuned-in. As you spiritually grow, you will know things you have no way of knowing. You may see energies or beings you've never seen before that exist outside of your belief system. This is such a beautiful gift but may seem scary at first, especially when it happens suddenly and out of the blue.

My personal experiences of my spiritual awakening are explained in my first book, You're Not Crazy, You're Simply Divine. A Guide to Help You Step into Your Soul's True Purpose. My experience was very surreal and unexpected. Suddenly, I could see through dimensions. It was like a thick veil had been lifted and I could see things that I had never experienced before. I could see the past just like it was in my current time and place. Some of the things I experienced were fascinating and exciting, and some things were terrifying. After learning from mentors, books, and friends, I concluded that I had more power if I used my inner light, and by doing so, nothing could harm me. I learned about the Angels and Spirit Guides, and how to call on them to help me anytime, anyplace. I then chose excitement and joy instead of fear, and it catapulted me into an amazing new experience in life, one where I can see between the veils of existence, time, and space while helping others on their path of living a life with much more substance and meaning.

Humans live multiple lifetimes to experience all forms of drama. We choose to come into each incarnation to experience highs and lows, and through those highs and lows, our souls expand and we learn at the deep soul level all the lessons that we choose. This helps us with soul growth. If you are reading this book, then you are seeking to remember and clear the veils of amnesia, lessons that you chose to experience here on Earth. When you heal and clear the low vibrational experiences, you will rise to a higher vibration. Each step upward helps you to fill your energy body with more light, allowing you to climb a spiritual staircase or ladder to a higher dimension. The more you do that, the more psychically in tune you become with your loving Spirit Guides, Helpers, ancestors, Angels, and Ascended Masters. They have knowledge and wisdom for you that will help you on your journey.

In this book, I will guide you through many lessons on tapping into your psychic abilities, and meeting your Spirit Guides, Angels, ancestors, and spiritual Helpers of light. You will learn who they are and why they are here. I will help you to release your inner shadows and demons, eventually shedding the old self which will help you emerge into the fresh, empowered self that you were born to be. You will learn how to raise your vibration, clear low energy, clear your past life blocks and traumas, and break down veils of energy that blind you from your psychic senses. I will help you safely discern what is of positive energy and how to feel with your intuitive senses what is not in your best interest so you can do this Divine work safely. I will also teach you about mediumship and connecting with people in spirit and how to cross over those who need help and have not yet crossed over into the light.

My biggest joy is to see every individual's spiritual gifts blossom and take shape. When you clear your shadows and emerge into each higher level of light, you access more of your Divine gifts and abilities. This happens in increments as you are ready to receive them. When your past lives are cleared and cleansed, you can energetically download the knowledge and gifts you have learned from mastery in other lifetimes. In essence, you are just opening up to your knowledge across space and time. This is such an awe-inspiring experience to have. It adds to the great mystery of life.

Please keep in mind that this book is entirely channeled by my Divine loving spiritual team of light, which includes many Ascended Masters, Angels, Archangels, spirit Helpers, and spirit animals. The information is from them and is my channeled teachings from them.

They show me that they work with each reader's spiritual guides to help you on your path to spiritual awakening and enlightenment.

As I have learned by reading dozens of books by other channelers and from classes taught by many teachers, every human has a belief system and Divine guidance that varies from one person to another. My Guides show me that the reason for those differences in opinion is that we all have our unique ways to channel Divine information. No two people are alike! We all have had experiences in life that differ from each other, and since this is how Spirit provides us the information, we see things differently and we comprehend things differently. Be patient. Learn to discern what is true to you. Take each lesson and see how it feels to you. If you know in your gut it isn't right for you, then it isn't. That is the beauty of this work. It is not all set in stone and with time moving forward, energy changes and shifts direction. As we move forward in time on Earth, energy moves and changes just like the tides of the ocean and like a beach that changes over time.

My channeled teachings are for everyone on a spiritual journey. It is not exclusively for people who want to be psychics or mediums. It is for anyone who wants to enrich their lives, learn how to connect to their true self, and uncover life's mysteries. You are here for a purpose, and your spiritual team is here to assist you whether you want to be a business owner, a cowboy, or a spiritual healer. Here on Earth, we are spiritual beings, ready to have an adventure, and you are a shining light in the Universe. You are a part of the whole universe, you are connected to the stars, to the planets, to each plant, flower, and mountain. You can connect and flow with the elements of air, earth, water, fire, and the Divine light of Source.

Thank you for joining me on this journey! I am excited to share my experiences and knowledge with you! It's so exciting to do this Divine work and I am so very blessed to connect with the Divine and so many of you on my journey. This work is always a learning lesson. Every day I do this sacred and blessed work. Daily, I learn something new. May this book help you discover that you are your own guru.

May your journey be filled with joy, magic, and excitement!

I'm so excited to guide you on this amazing adventure!

Namaste,

Kathleen Sherman

What is a Psychic Medium?

Chapter 2

What is a Psychic Medium? Let's Get Started with Important Tips and Exercises to Strengthen Your Energy Body.

There are many different types of psychic abilities, and each human has a unique style of receiving that psychic information from Spirit. Our uniqueness is our biggest attribute! The truth is that we all have many psychic abilities. All humans are intuitive, psychic beings and have the ability to communicate with Spirits, each other, plants, animals, and the Universe itself! My Higher-Self shows me that we come from the same source of light, or God-spark of light then split into our over-soul, then split again into our Higher Self, then into the crown chakra, or energy center of our human body. We also have energy centers on the Earth, which connect us from above and below. Below our feet is the Earth star chakra, and at the base of the Earth is the Earth gateway chakra, connecting us to Divine mother energy located in deep Earth.

What is the definition of psychic? From Merriam-Webster Dictionary, the definition of psychic is

> *1: of or relating to the psyche: PSYCHOGENIC*

> *2: lying outside the sphere of physical science or knowledge: immaterial, moral, or spiritual in origin or force*

3: sensitive to nonphysical or supernatural forces and influences: marked by extraordinary or mysterious sensitivity, perception, or understanding

Definition of psychic (Entry 2 of 2)

1a: a person apparently sensitive to nonphysical forces. (Merriam-Webster n.d.)

What is the definition of mediumship? From Merriam-Webster Dictionary the definition of mediumship is

the capacity, function, or profession of a spiritualistic medium. (Merriam-Webster n.d.)

What is my spirit team's definition of psychic?

Psychic ability is a message you receive that somehow flows into your mind easily. It is a funny little joke that floats in like a friend is telling you, but you can't always see who it is. It is knowing what is coming in the future, and how things may turn out for someone. It's a culmination of the gifts of the Clairs that give you messages of hope and direction for you and others. It's knowing what is on the other side of a flash card or knowing what the weather will be that day.

What is my spirit team's definition of mediumship?

Mediumship is the ability to communicate with those who have crossed over (passed away) from the physical realm. We, as humans, are also able to communicate with people who have not crossed over by means of speaking with them through the mind and consciousness. For example, I have been able to communicate clearly with living animals, people in a coma, people on the spectrum who are non-verbal, people who were in a sleep state, and people who were on drugs and in a different dimension. I was also able to communicate with my mother when I was a baby through the mind. I feel like most mothers can tap into this ability.

There are many different dimensions that people can travel to. Sometimes in altered mental states, like drug-induced states, they can be lost but still be here on Earth in a physical body.

There are many different Spirit Guides, Angels, Ascended Masters, ancestors, and such that are guiding us and providing us with messages. To me, all this would be considered mediumship. It is communication with others, whether they are on the Earth plane or elsewhere.

Quick note: this does not mean that you need to "see" the spirit or person (clairvoyance) you are communicating with. The communication could be connecting you through any of the Clairs such as hearing the spirit (clairaudience), feeling (clairsentience), or a deep knowing of who it is (claircognizance).

The Clairs

The five Clairs are as follows and are the main ways you may experience intuitive messages from your spiritual team. Our spiritual helpers and team are always trying to give us helpful information. They must go through dimensional veils to convey information to us and they get that information through to us in any way they can. It's like trying to connect with someone who can't hear or see, and they have to be very imaginative to get the messages through to us when we aren't as open spiritually. This is like a game of charades. When I'm doing mediumship work with clients, which is speaking to spirit, they most often show me how they are trying to communicate with their loved ones. Quite often, their loved ones don't get the message or they don't believe it is real.

As the vibration on Earth rises to higher frequencies, more people are receiving these messages. They may try to connect with us while we are awake or asleep.

The five psychic Clairs are:

Clairvoyance – inner seeing, this is connected to the third eye chakra. You may see in your mind's eye in the form of visions, or you may see with your physical eyes.

Clairsentience – the ability to receive intuitive messages via feelings, emotions, or physical sensations.

Clairaudience – clear hearing, which may be through the ears (which are chakras), or through the head like a loudspeaker. This may feel like a thought in your mind or it may be the voice of someone else.

Claircognizance – clear knowing of something you have no knowledge of or recollection of.

Clairsalience – clear smelling. This is common with cologne, food, smoke, or a type of flower to give you a message from a loved one.

Clairgustance – clear tasting. You may have a sudden sense of taste which is also a way your Spirit Guides give you information.

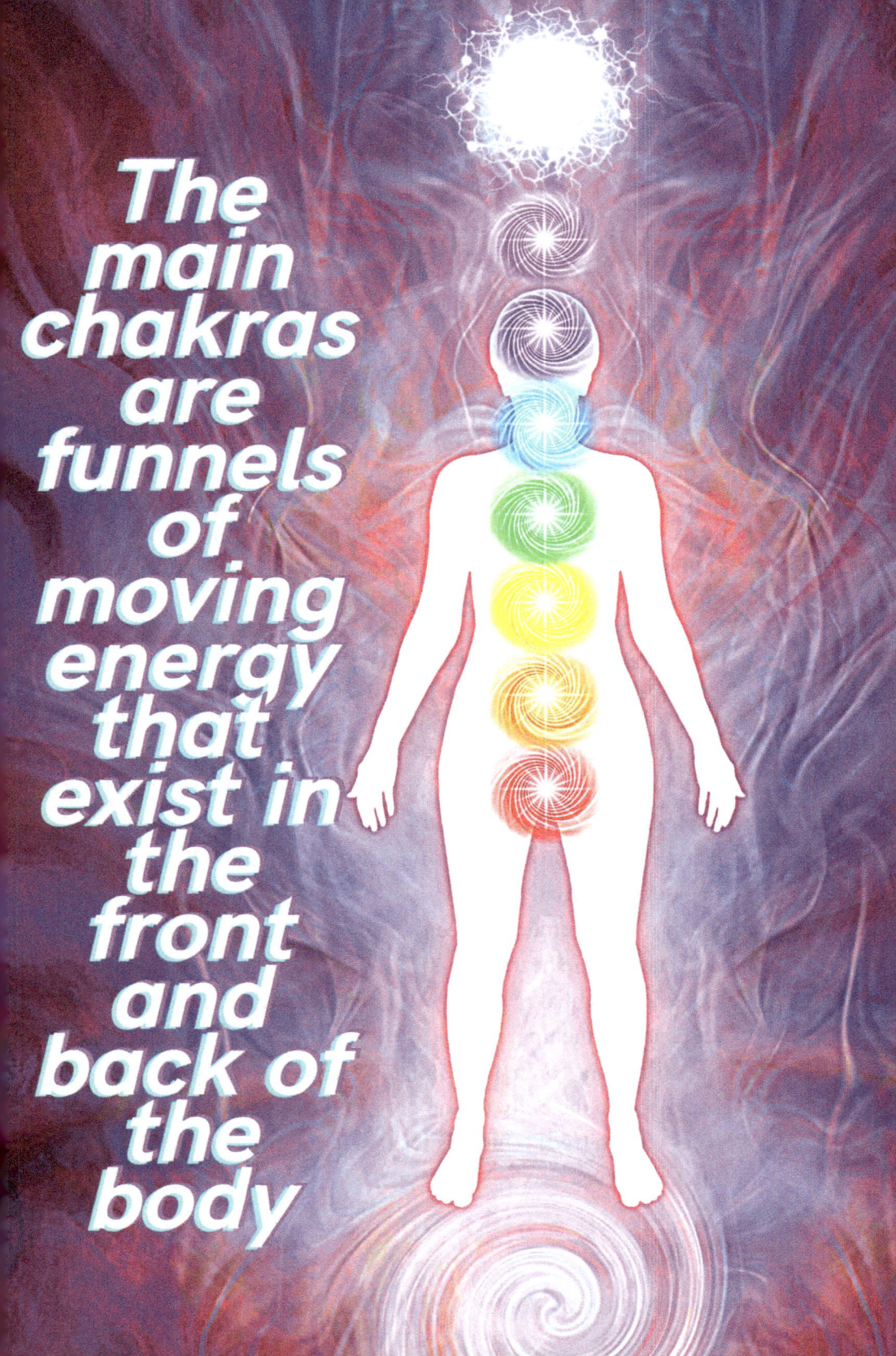

The main chakras are funnels of moving energy that exist in the front and back of the body

Bonus Content

The Chakras

The chakra system is the energy center that flows source energy from the heavens through our crown, located at the top of our head. I picture a large funnel situated at the top of my head, funneling source energy into my body through my crown chakra. This connects to the pineal gland in our head and flows light energy and information into our minds. This energy flows through our bodies, then through the seven main chakras, and finally into the Earth.

The main seven chakras are as follows:

Crown chakra (violet) – located at the top of the head with the funnel open to the heavens.

Third eye chakra (indigo) – funnels located in the front and back, middle of the forehead.

Throat chakra (light blue) – funnels located in the front and back of the throat.

Heart chakra (emerald green) – funnels located in the front and back of the heart.

Solar Plexus chakra (yellow) – funnels located in the front and back of the upper belly.

Sacral chakra (orange) – funnels located in the front and back, below the belly button.

Root chakra (red) – funnels located in the front and back of the low pelvis.

All of us have over 100 energy centers, called chakras, in our bodies including our joints, pressure points, sinuses, palms, and feet. You may see them in your mind's eye as spinners of energy, lotus flowers spinning, or in any way, your inner sight shows you. If those chakras are not spinning in a clockwise fashion, you may have an energy block in your auric field. There is also a tube of light that flows through the middle of the chakra centers from Heaven to Earth, and that is called the prana tube, or central channel. This tube of light helps run Divine energy from the heavens through your body, into the Earth, and then back up through the body to the heavens.

~~~

Exercise

Learn to Run Your Energy
with the Divine

You can focus in with your mind's eye, and using your breath, create a ball of light in any color you can imagine. With your breath, move that ball of light up and down through that channel. With your "in" breath, breathe Divine white light energy from above, down through the tube in the center of your body, and move the glowing ball of light down through that channel, through your body, and into the Earth. On your "out" breath, flow the energy up and down thus connecting you to the Heavens and the Earth. Send the energy up and down through your body until it feels like it's running on its own. Then tell your cellular body (talk to yourself and give it instructions) to keep running all the time this way. This is called running your energy!

~~~

Exercise

Learn to Ground Your Energy

Grounding your energy body is one of the most important things to learn. If you are not spiritually grounded into the Earth through your feet, then you don't have the connection complete from Heaven to Earth. You can do this by creating roots that grow downwards from your body, deep into the Earth, like a plant or a tree. You can do this by using your breath and focusing in your mind's eye on growing those roots deep into the Earth and anchoring them in. If you don't psychically "see" with your mind's eye well, then just tell your energy to do what you'd like it to. Try your best to use all your senses to move energy from Heaven to Earth and through the ground and anchor them deep into Mother Earth. Pay attention to any feelings of movement in the physical body. When you are firmly grounded to the Earth, release any energy that isn't healthy for you, directing it into the Earth. Another few ways of grounding your energy to the Earth is by creating an energy ball of green light (any color you'd like will work) and sending it into the Earth through the central channel. Ground it into the Earth in the same way as the roots. You may also walk outside barefoot on the ground or put your hands in the dirt, put your hands on a tree, or whatever feels right to you. As a medical intuitive, I see many people who aren't grounded, and it looks like their feet are flying up. They may be flighty, can't make a decision, and don't feel safe.

~~~

Run your energy like a fountain from the ground up!

Exercise

Become a Fountain of Shimmering Light!

Another way of grounding your energy is by running it up from the Earth through your body, through the chakras, and out your head. Then, send that energy up into the heavens and expand it out and down around you. This field of energy is called the toroidal field, and it looks like you are the center of a fountain. Create a colorful fountain of energy that energetically lights your energy body and fills you with Divine energy from Mother Earth. I love to create this in many colors, and you can change the colors as they go up through the chakra system. Use your breath to breathe the energy up from the Earth, breathe out when it goes up into the heavens, and then rain the energy around you and back into the Earth. This clears your energy field and builds a light barrier through your energy body within your physical body and the auric field that surrounds you. This helps to keep your Merkaba, or energy body, very strong like a shield of multicolored light. It acts as a force field of light and keeps you safe from low vibrational entities and energies.

~~~

VIOLET FLAME

USING THE VIOLET FLAME WILL TRANSMUTE NEGATIVE ENERGY

Exercise

Clearing Yourself and Your Sacred Space: Archangel Gabriel

Archangel Gabriel's name means messenger of God. He works with the violet flame and works with communication. The violet flame transmutes any low vibrational energies. Fill your body and home with this energy to clear it from harsh energies, and to cleanse and uplift your body, mind, and sacred space. Call on him to help you with your emotional state. He is compassionate and caring and will give you guidance in your spiritual journey.

~~~

Exercise

Safety First! What to NEVER Forget! Intention and Setting Your Sacred Space

This paragraph contains one of the most important things I can say. Please don't forget- no matter what you are doing in the world of spirit and the esoteric.

You are the creator of your experiences, and it is very important to set some boundaries with Spirit. Before jumping in and speaking with Spirit, working with Spirit, or doing ANY kind of divination such as pendulum, oracle cards, or tarot cards, work on setting your intentions of who and what you allow into your space. If you don't set boundaries before you begin to channel, you are leaving yourself open to many types of entities, energies, demons, and human spirits. Those who are naturally more open to Spirit can unknowingly allow in whatever decides to come around while you are opening up. I will explain this more in Chapter 3.

~~~

Create sacred space, and set healthy boundaries

Chapter 3

Create Sacred Space for You, Within Your Space, and Setting Healthy Boundaries

Every human on Earth is born a superhero. We are all Divine beings of light that choose to come into a human body to have an extraordinary experience. We choose our emotional disposition, and physical attributes, and choose our bodies in accordance with what we would like to experience on Earth. We also choose our story line or outline of the experiences we would like to have while here. When we come into the body, we go through a veil of amnesia, resulting in our inability to recollect all our other existences and lifetimes that we've experienced. Many humans have experienced hundreds of lifetimes here on Earth, and many from other planets and solar systems. If you are reading this book, then you probably have as well.

In the following chapters, I will help you work on issues and fears that may arise or already exist for you while tapping into the world of spirit.

The first thing to do is set your intentions in greater detail, being more specific with what types of energy and who is allowed in your space. When you are doing this work, you must realize that you are a sacred being of light. You are Divine! You are made up of only Divine light. You were born in this Divine light and made purely of that light. Being on Earth and experiencing hard situations and environments dulls this light. It is important to clear your energy and set your intentions and boundaries within your personal space.

When you use divination tools such as tarot, oracle cards, or a pendulum, you open a space that opens a portal for whatever you intend it to be open for. Before doing any of this work, your intentions should be set in stone with your Angels. Make a statement in your mind or say it out loud:

I only allow those who walk in the light of Source to communicate with me and to be in my sacred space.

You only need to say this once, either in your mind or out loud for your team of light to hear you and understand. You may come up with your own wording to set your intentions. Many different modalities can be used to set intentions, and each modality is different. For example, some use a circle around their body with either salt or a candle. If you choose to energetically draw a circle around your body, then you can also set the intention that only beings of light and love are allowed to cross the threshold. You may also do this in your home or business. You may always call upon your Angels and Spirit Helpers (even if you don't know who they are yet) to help with this task. That is what they are there for!

I have experienced many clients who did not set their intentions and, because of this, it directly resulted in negative spiritual attachments. It is a simple and quick thought to your spiritual team of light. You can tell them once and set it as a standing intention that is set until further notice. The divination tool I have seen the worst experiences with is the Ouija board. This can be a positive tool if the person has the correct training with them. The Ouija board acts as a portal that allows very negative entities to enter by opening portals in the space. This can cause haunting. Unless you know, and I mean really know, what you are doing, I do not recommend playing with them. I strongly suggest you do not go near them.

I have also seen this with tarot cards, but this could have easily been avoided by setting the intention prior to starting the reading. Tarot cards, oracle cards, and pendulums can be very helpful in opening your spiritual potential. They act as assistants to spark your intuition. There are many other helpful tools for divination. As long as you have set your intention, the sky is the limit!

What are Negative Spiritual Attachments?

There are many types of spiritual beings, some can be negative, and some can be positive. There is no Hell, but the human race has been made to fear it with the thoughts of fire, brimstone, and burning for eternity. The devil was created by Mankind to keep us preoccupied with the fear of sin and the Devil. Why? Because if you are in fear, you can't connect with the Divine aspect of self. I have journeyed and worked with the Divine for years. There are Demons and Angels. There is an opposite to everything except the God-Source. It was all created by our Divine Creator to create contrast and for us to live our lives, learn, and have many different experiences. I clear demons and lower vibrational negative entities, shadow energy figures (energy called thought forms, which look to me like smoky dark energy), and I assist spirit humans to the light if they are willing. I will also guide you to work with your spiritual guides and Angels to help keep you safe. They will clear negative energies for you and keep them away from you. Every human has the ability to clear negative entities, but for now, I will teach you to ask your spiritual team for assistance. If you ask, they will watch over you and keep you safe.

Set your intention in stone with your spiritual team by setting these boundaries. Angels and Helpers are there waiting for you to connect with them. When I work with clients and tell them their Angels and Spirit Helpers are there, the Angels and Spirit Helpers quite often show me they are having a huge party because they are so excited and happy to connect. They work all our lives to get us to connect and listen to them.

Please note: if you are a person who doesn't do well setting boundaries in life, then you may have the same problem with Spirit. I see it as a lesson in standing up for yourself and not allowing yourself to be a push-over. This experience may bleed into all areas of your life until you learn this lesson.

This may mean that when you say you only allow beings of light into your space, and you don't feel confident that you have the power to say that, then it simply won't work. If you really believe your words, then it will be so, because you truly believe in yourself.

This teaches you to set boundaries, and to hold steady with them. So be firm and confident, and step into your power when you make these statements to Spirit.

~~~

Exercise

Creating Sacred Space

1. Make sure your space feels loving and free of harsh energy. To create your sacred space, you may light candles and incense, put on esoteric music, smudge with sage, and fill the room with salt lamps, crystals, diffuse essential oils, or whatever makes you feel content.

2. Close your eyes, take a deep breath, and fill your body with Divine light from an opening in the heavens that floods your light body and flows into the Earth.

3. Extend that energy to the whole room or space you are in. Intend that the whole sky opens to rain Divine light and energy throughout the entire space. Allow that energy to wash away any energetic residue that may be there.

4. Sit in the lotus position (cross-legged with palms up on each knee) or lie down in a comfortable place with no animals or possible interruptions.

5. Ask for your high vibrational Spirit Helpers of the Divine light to come in and assist you. You may call on your loving Spirit Guides, Angels, high vibrational ancestors that are in the light, and power animals of light.

6. Ask for protection from your Angels from anything that is not of the highest vibration of the Source/Creator. Ask them to

surround you with a cushion of light from them to keep anything far away from you and your sacred energy field.

7. Pay attention to a feeling of comfort and bliss that surrounds you from your Angels and your spiritual team of light.

8. Thank them all, ground your energy through your feet, and send your grounding cord into the Earth. Bring your energy back to your heart and feel a lovely green glow that comes from your own heart.

9. Open your eyes and come back to the room.

CHAPTER 4

Raise your vibration

Chapter 4

Raising Vibration and Spiritual Antennae: How to Connect and Tune Your Channeling Rod! This is Connected to Your Empathic Abilities.

We are all intuitive beings of light and are made up of spinning chakras of energy that flow through the meridians of the energy body and the central channel. The central channel is like a straw that guides and directs this energy through the body. The central channel can also be described as a spiritual antenna, connecting you to the Divine above, below, and around you. Surrounding the outside of the body, this spiritual antenna resembles white, soft flowing feelers, protruding around the body like little hairs, extending from the top of the head (crown chakra). In my mind's eye, I am shown that it looks like a television antenna. This connection runs all through the body and down into the Earth. I also see this as a tree with roots at the top and the bottom. We are the messengers and the bridge between the Heavens and Earth. I am also shown that this is how we plug in.

To access this antenna, you use your mind's eye, or conscious thought to see, feel, or know and connect it to the Divine above and below. These spiritual antennae are how you feel the energy from Spiritual Helpers, other humans, animals, and nature.

Through these antennae, humans feel the energy from each other. Please take a few minutes to close your eyes and envision what that may look like in your mind's eye. Those antennae are feelers that move energy from other humans, animals, trees, and the Earth. Follow the vision or feeling of energy from a tree. We are consciously connected to everything on Earth. Every tree, plant, rock, and animal have an energy that is like ours and has the same feelers. It's much like the roots of a tree under the Earth, and the energy from the roots goes to the next tree and the next, forming a web of energy that is pulsating and moving constantly. The energy weaves itself and forms a communication network through plant life. We have that as well but have been disconnected from it in many ways. We are in the age of awakening, and we are now learning that we are connected to everything and everyone.

You may experience that when you are around others and are feeling energies, good or bad, emotions, pain, joy, excitement, or anger. Your psychic feelers that are interconnected to theirs bring that energy into your conscious awareness.

When this happens, you are experiencing psychic empathy. You feel, sense, smell, taste, or know what that person is experiencing through your light body. Some people may even experience hearing thoughts from others.

You can work with your Angels and Spirit Guides to help you balance this spiritual gift. It can be overwhelming at times. Simply ask them!

Please note: you don't have to live with being overwhelmed with your empathic abilities. You can set your intentions with your guides to tone this down, just like a tuner or button that can be created in your mind's eye or consciousness. Working with your auric field, you can reduce and limit the number of negative feelings and emotions that you allow in from others. And yes, I said allow. What you say out loud or in your mind also sets those boundaries. Simply state in your mind or out loud what you would like to experience. You have a say in how this works and what you like and don't like. You can say to your guides, 'Thank you, I got the message, now please take this energy away'. You may also say, 'Thank you. Now I release what is not my energy'. Take a deep breath in and as you exhale, that energy can be released immediately along with it, if it is not your own energy.

For example, I often feel a client's physical or emotional pain in my body. It can feel like instant anxiety or fear. Other times, I may feel a physical pain or ache in my body, or a heaviness. This can be coming from someone alive or in spirit. This is how we are given information on how someone is feeling. This helps me with my work and helps others to heal their bodies and the auric field. I have learned that this is a powerful tool to have as it allows me to understand what that person is going through. It's important to pay attention to your own body and energy to see if what you are feeling is your energy or someone else's.

~~~

Exercise

Connect Your Spiritual Antenna or Rod of Divinity! Part 1

1. Set your intention and open your sacred space. Make sure you are comfortable and call in your spiritual team of light.

2. Flood your light body with Divine light from the Heavens. Set the intention that you are open to the most loving connection with the Divine above and below. The sky opens with a beautiful pole of light and an anchor that is connected to the most amazing light in the heavens. It travels down into your crown chakra when you take a deep breath in. Breathe this light from the heavens through your central channel, down through your root chakra at the pelvis, and down into the Earth. Use your mind's eye to envision that light turning into a spinning spiral that anchors deep into the Earth. Out the sides of that pole of light, expand tree roots out, deep into the Earth, extending many out into the Earth. Use your breath and consciousness to create those roots. These are the feelers that I have already explained.

3. Now you feel grounded and this Divine energy from the Heavens is coming down through the central channel and there is a spiral around it, constantly flowing that energy through your body. It also sends Divine delicious energy all through your body, through your arms, and legs.

4. Bring that energy back up through your crown chakra, back up to the Divine light above, and plug into that light. Allow yourself to breathe in that amazing, all-knowing light of source. Allow it to permeate into every part of your being. Your Angels then wrap their wings around you and hold you for as long as you like.

5. Thank your Angels and ride the wave of bliss back down into your crown chakra, breathing your way back down into your body, into the center of your heart space.

6. Ground your energy into the Earth again and feel the little hair-like antennae that come out of your energy body come out into the space around you.

7. Set your intention that you only allow your energy to connect with the Divine and only Spirit who walks in the white light.

8. Come back to yourself, ground back into your physical body, which is now glowing with radiating Divine light.

9. Ask your Angels to help you put a ring of golden light around your auric field to transmute lower vibrations from others. See it in your mind's eye or feel it in your energy.

10. Thank your spiritual team of light for helping you plug in. Come back to the room.

~~~

Exercise

Tuning Your Spiritual Antennae, Your Connection to the Divine, and Vibration. Part 2

Your spiritual antennae are connected to the flow of Divine light from Source and Mother Earth. You can tune it like a radio or television. If the energy is too strong, it may feel overwhelming to you. It may feel like your head is in the clouds or full of loving and strong energy. The trick to tuning is to call on your Spiritual Guides and Helpers to come and assist you in setting the energetic station of your spiritual antennae. You do this with your breath and consciousness.

1. Call on your high vibrational spirit Helpers of light, Angels, Spirit Guides, and Helpers.

2. Ask them to assist you in setting your energy to the exact setting that is perfect for you.

3. In your mind's eye, create a dial or equalizer button that slides up and down for volume. At the top is 100 percent, and at the bottom is 0. I am teaching this lesson with the visual of the equalizer button. If you choose a dial, simply use that visual instead.

4. These buttons are also in Hermetic teaching (Hermes Trismegistus, who was a great spiritual teacher in ancient Egypt)

called poles of polarity. You choose what frequency you like your energy to be set to.

5. With your conscious thought, envision that there is a small ball of light that moves the polarity up and down with your thoughts and breath. To play with this energy, take a deep breath in and move the ball with your thoughts and breath.

6. With the breath in, move the ball up to 100 percent with your thoughts and energy. Feel an immense feeling of light, love, and acceptance within every cell of your being. Stay there for as long as you like.

7. Next, take another breath in, and on the breath out, send that ball down to 50 percent, stay there for a few minutes, and feel the energy lessen. Notice how that energy shift feels different in your body and mind.

8. After you are done at 50 percent, breathe in again and on the out-breath, send the ball to the zero point at the bottom. Feel the energy in that space. All the Divine flooding love energy from Source is now shut off.

9. After these exercises, you now know what it feels like to feel the Source connection with the Divine at full connection, half connection, and zero connection.

10. Use your breath again to bring that up to the perfect setting for you to live in most of the time. Set the intention that you lock it into place with your team of light. You may envision a lock or some sort in your mind's eye. Most people set their pole of vibration above the half point. I keep mine set at 87 percent most of the time.

11. Important note: you will want to set your pole at a level that feels centered and calm. For daily life in the 3D world, you will want to stay balanced. If you feel like your head is in the clouds all the time, you may have difficulties staying focused.

12. When you choose to meditate or to do spiritual work, then reset your percentage. Make sure to always reset to your normal vibratory state you set up with this exercise.

From the Book The Kybalion, According to Hermes Trismegistus's Teachings

The Principle of Mentalism:
1. The all is mind; the Universe is mental.
2. The Principal of Correspondence: As Above, So Below; As Within, So Without; As the Universe, So the Soul.
3. The Principle of Vibration: Nothing rests; Everything moves; Everything vibrates.
4. The Principle of Polarity: Everything is dual; Everything has poles.
5. The Principle of Rhythm: Everything flows, out and in; Everything has its tides; All things rise and fall.
6. The Principle of Cause and Effect: Every cause has its effect; Every effect has its cause.
7. The Principle of Gender: Gender is in everything; Everything has its masculine and feminine principles.

There are poles of polarity to many aspects of life for each individual. You create energy with your thoughts, and that is how you move that ball of light around in your body. It is your conscious thought and the energy with your breath that moves it. You can look inside your polarities and see where your mindset is on many different topics.

You may choose to look at where your pole is set for the money, love, psychic gifts, and many more. Use your awareness to ask your spiritual team to help you to see where you are set on these poles.

For example, look at love. From zero to 100, where are you set now? What pops into your mind? Are you able to see in your mind's eye where you are set now? If you feel it is low, then that may explain why you have a hard time with loving relationships.

Next, look at self-confidence. Where do you feel you are now? How about abundance, safety, or spiritual psychic abilities? Create a pole for each one, which ends up looking like an equalizer, with many poles of polarity. Create your own! This is a fun exercise that you can do all by yourself.

You can use the tools you just learned to move them up the ladder to 80 percent, or even 100 percent. These being up to the top is perfect! Make sure you lock into the new higher level. This exercise also shows you some inner work that may need to be done.

Don't forget to thank your spiritual team of light.

Start Your Journal

Begin a journal that you can refer to with dates to see your progress in the future. Write down what you find within your energetic poles. What do you need to work on? What are your findings? I recommend starting a mediumship journal now with all your valuable information.

Chapter 5

How To Recieve Psychic Information

Chapter 5

Psychic Abilities and How You May Receive Psychic Information. Tools From Spirit.

There are unlimited ways you may receive psychic information. Your Spiritual Guides and Helpers are tirelessly working to send you information that will help you on your path in life. As I've said before, they use what they can in your human experience to give you, their assistance. In my experience, my Guides give me phrases from movies, books, and songs. They love to make me laugh and I feel like I'm talking to wonderful friends and laughing at a joke that no one else can hear. That's what your Guides are – friends! Many of our Spirit Guides are friends or other aspects of self that are guiding us along our journey here on Earth. They have had many incarnations and have the knowledge and spiritual maturity to take that role on for us. We choose them, and they choose to assist us. Many times, it can feel like you are in the dark and have no one there. They are there, beyond that veil, cheering us on, encouraging us, and showing us the way to the light. They are there to help us as humans to have the experience we chose to have while here. They lead us to experiences that may seem harsh at times but lead us to experiences that give us the most soul growth. They also help us to move through those experiences and overcome, forgive, and move on. When you feel like you're in the dark and no one is there, ask them to step in, turn on the light, and help you through the hard times.

Tools for Intuition from My Divine Team of Light and Yours

1. Allow the Information.

Do you feel you are worthy of Divine assistance? This is what my team is saying is the Number 1 block for humans. You are worthy of Divine love and help. Set the intention and permit yourself to receive Divine assistance from your Divine team of light.

2. Receive Information, Don't Push it Away.

You are a version of a specialized radio receiver that is built for receiving Divine love, light, and information. The energetic human body is composed of a crystalline substance that flows Divine light and energy through it. Allow the information that is sent to you from Divine Helpers to come in easily as the way it was created. If you work at getting that information, then you are pushing energy away from you. It is simple. Allow it to flow in effortlessly.

I simply set the intention that I allow Divine messages to flow in with my breath through my crystalline energy system. Let it flow through, and as it flows, it brings the messages in with ease.

3. We Send the Information Like a Lightning Bolt.

Your spirit team sends quick messages to you. This is very accurate information that they give us, whether it is through a quick knowing, hearing, or with visual information. Most humans don't trust instant knowledge and then question it. My Guides always make me laugh when I do this because they show me that they work so hard to get me and others this lightning bolt of knowledge, and we brush it off. They get very frustrated and roll their eyes to show me how we ignore the work they do. They ask that you learn to trust that instant knowing that you may have. It will save you a lot of worries. When you learn to trust your instinct and the instant message, you will stop questioning that information. When you question the message, you twist it up with what your human mind changes it into. Information comes in crisp and precise. Don't change it or dream up interpretations. Allow what is given exactly the way it is presented and thank them for that knowledge. That precise information has a specific meaning, and it's not meant to be interpreted. When you think it makes no sense, it should make perfect sense to someone else. This happens to me often when I don't have a clue why I'm given a detail or a word. But for someone else, this quick message is how Spirit is giving them proof of a loved one, a specific situation, or an experience for that person.

4. Take Yourself and Your Ego Out of the Picture.

We all have an ego and it helps us in life, but it also hinders us. The ego was made to keep us safe but also gets bruised and mistreated. Pay attention to your self-talk and how you feel about yourself. If you notice negative self-talk, your ego is affected by this. Close your eyes and feel if your ego is balanced, or out of balance. Picture your ego in your mind's eye. What does it look like? What does your ego feel like? If it is out of balance, you have some work to do in healing that ego. You can begin by changing your self-talk. We will work on this in the next chapter about shadow work.

Take your feelings, emotions, and bias out of the picture. Messages from the Divine do not have anything to do with your feelings. If you are looking for a message that you are emotionally connected to, then you may not get a clear message. Your own emotions may alter what Spirit is giving you. If you put your emotions completely to the side and reconnect with Source, then you will be able to channel a message that is not distorted.

5. We Reach You Through Your Senses and Through Your Emotional Body.

Spirit has ways of making us feel very intense emotions. Human spirits make me feel the most emotions, especially if they have not crossed over to the light. Human spirits have the choice of crossing over to the light (Source or to God). Those who have not yet crossed into the light haven't been cleared of the human emotional experience and still have unhealed emotions. When channeling a human spirit in this form, you will feel all the emotions they still carry. It can be overwhelming. Also, these spirits may not always be kind. They may feel heavier in energy, and you may feel those emotions yourself. If you feel this is the case, ask them to leave your energy field. They will do so immediately.

Human spirits that have crossed over to the light feel much lighter and bring helpful messages. They are still the same soul. They may have a brighter outlook because they have gone through many stages of healing and detoxifying from their human experience, unlike those who have not crossed the veil yet. I will go into more detail on human spirits later in the book. You can choose to work with only those who have crossed to the light.

Your Spirit Guides and Helpers also send loving energy and knowledge through your emotional body. They are experts in helping you to receive wisdom. They use feelings of joy for an uplifting feeling, and the chills when you are on track. When Spirit gives us chills or shivers, they are dancing, clapping, and cheering you on. This is what that feels like. I get visions of my client's team of light having a big party and sending them uplifting feelings of joy and bliss.

Your Guides can be trusted, and as you open more and more, you may feel this more in your emotional body. Feelings of joy, immense love, and support come along with the messages they send you. I cry with many messages from spirits that have crossed, and from Spirit Guides. It is a beautiful energy and love they send through you, the messenger, to the recipient of the message.

6. How do You Differentiate Between Self-Talk and Messages From the Divine?

This is one of the biggest questions I get from clients. The message comes from outside of you, from above, from the side. When you get a spiritual message, check in with yourself first. *Was that my thought? Did I create that thought?* If not, then it is a message from your Spirit Guides or a human spirit. If you state that you only allow those who walk in the white light to speak to you, then you know it is your Helpers or a spirit that has crossed over and is helping you.

I noticed one day that I heard with my right ear, and within my head, dialogue coming in like I was talking to myself and answering myself as well. I questioned this and realized that the voice speaking back to me referred to me as *"you"* instead of *"I"*. If I had been responding to my physical self in my mind, I would have said "I". This experience taught me to pay attention to the information I was receiving. After that day, I knew it was my Spirit Guides talking to me.

7. We Give You Signs From the Universe. Pay Attention!

Spirit laughs when they say this because humans ignore their signs the most. Signs from your Angels and Spirit Guides are everywhere. You just need to notice them. Your Guides have a special way of making you look at something when there is only a split-second left to see it. These are packed with meaning for you. These messages also may come from loved ones who have crossed over and want you to know they are safe and they are with you.

Spiritual signs come through billboards, license plates, numbers (numerology), and animals such as birds, butterflies, and dragonflies. There was one instance where my daughter Sierra had a butterfly land on her shirt for a very long time.

We all had the loving feeling of my mother right away, with a knowing that she was there with us enjoying a sunny day. She was making her presence known.

Signs may come through social media, technology, or something that a friend mentions in a chat. Your spiritual team organizes those messages for the exact right timing.

My mother is wonderful at having a specific song play right when I needed to hear the words of encouragement from the song. She also leaves dimes for family members.

8. We Study Your Habits and Put Helpers on Your Path for Awareness.

Your spiritual guidance team watches you and helps create experiences such as the ones I mentioned. This takes strategic work to create these signs from the Universe. Thank them when you notice the signs.

9. We Love to Stay Up to Date with World Experiences.

Spirit Helpers love to stay up to date with what is going on in the world. They use technology to bring you the most up-to-date messages. For example, my Guides began by giving me emoji pictures in my mind's eye for answers when I began. They used a thumbs up, or a smiley face for yes, and a thumbs down or sad face for no. At times, I would see a generic head in my mind's eye nodding yes or no. At times, I still get yeses and noes in this way from my Guides, but I have leveled up where I hear the messages, which is much easier.

10. Quit Expecting Proof. It Will Show Up When You Least Expect It.

When I began working with Spirit, I felt the need to prove everything. Spirit will assist you and give you proof. It will come naturally. I noticed that the more I relaxed and quit worrying about proof, it came through much easier. My Guides explain that we put up energetic blocks when we worry about anything, especially that of proof. They will give you everything you need to prove that you are getting Divine information.

You will be much more accurate with your intuition if you allow it to free flow in, so do your best to allow it to flow in easily and have fun doing it! This is meant to be fun!

11. Why Are We Here? You Asked Us To! You Need Us, and We Need You.

Your Spirit Guides and Helpers are there because you made a contract with them. They scratch your back, and you scratch theirs! Human spirits acting as Guides gives them soul purpose and help them learn how to help others. They in turn help you when you may feel you are in the dark, and no one is there with you. All energy should be reciprocated, and this is a wonderful example of how we are all interconnected. We are multidimensional beings, meaning we have many parts of our soul that are all working at once to incarnate into different lifetimes, act as Spirit Guides for others, and attend spiritual schools to learn how to live in a more conscious state. Just like Jesus can be in many places at once, so can we.

12. Relax and Have Fun with Us! We Are Family.

Your spiritual team is your family. We come into lifetimes in soul groups to learn from each other and play all types of roles in each one. We choose these experiences and custom-create them. Your Spirit Guides may be other aspects of you from other lifetimes that learned hard lessons and can help you in this lifetime. They may also be family members such as a grandmother, parent, guardian, or friend. Many of our Spirit Helpers and Guides are decided upon before you come to Earth. We will work on meeting your team in this book. All humankind is family, but your Guides have been with you for lifetimes, and you have learned many lessons from each other.

13. Are You Open? If Not, Please Clear Your Fears and Beliefs on How This Works.

Clearing your fears opens the door. Lower vibrational feelings and emotions such as anger, fear, and anxiety shut the door from the spirit world and you. If you are afraid of messages or afraid of the world of spirit, then it may not be time for you to be doing this. If you are afraid, then I suggest you do some spiritual house cleaning to find out what it is that makes you fearful. There may be something or many things that are making you fearful of doing this work.

14. When You Relax, You Allow Divine Guidance.

Spirit is waiting for you to let down your guards to give you messages. This is why you get little light bulbs of clarity when you aren't busy. I began to notice this in my life when I was in the bathroom, or just walking through my house, and especially when I was working out. I began to notice that I would get ideas that would pop into my mind when nothing specific was on my mind and I was in a light trance-like state. Have you noticed that you may "space" out at times? This is a different level of consciousness that you can learn to go into. While running, walking, or working out, I go into this state of mind the most. This is where my ancestors (in my case, my parents) were able to speak to me. I now know that all my life when I was "spacing out", I was really downloading precious information from Source! That precious information is knowledge, wisdom, Divine messages, and pictures that help me see, feel, hear, or know information from the Divine. This also happens in between sleep states, especially before I wake up in the morning.

15. We Find a Way in Through What YOU THINK is Your Imagination.

Your imagination is the tool that helps you open your natural psychic intuitive abilities.

When you receive these downloads of Divine intuition and messages from your Divine team, it may feel as though it is just a figment of your imagination. Your imagination and inner childlike part of yourself is what allows that information to flow in. I channeled a spirit who was a male musician that showed me that when he played his music, he stepped into the flow of white light. He showed me that he "stepped out of that light" and could "step back into" that tube of light. When he played, he was flooded with it, and he called that "being in the flow."

Now in this time of higher vibration, we can stay in that flow all the time!

16. Stay in the Flow of Divine Light and Learn to Tune into Our Station.

Ask your Guides to assist you in always staying in the flow and use your consciousness to set your station and tuners. This helps you stay in the flow, activate your light body, keep your energy flowing at all times, and feel like a million bucks! It helps you cleanse out negative energy from others while keeping your energy body sparkling clean. Think of it as a shower of Divine light that you don't leave, you can simply control the shower of energy from a slow trickle to a full, drenching shower.

17. IMPORTANT NOTE: A fellow psychic friend once said to me, "I'm a psychic, I don't know everything!"

My friend was right! You don't and won't necessarily know every detail of everything when getting intuitive information. Spirit gives you exactly what they want, and sometimes you are not supposed to understand what it means. Simply give that person your channeled message. It should make sense to them. If they choose to include you in what it means to them, then that is their decision. You simply are a messenger to help give them the Aha! moment and let them know there is something mystical that is beyond their scope of imagination!

When I was awakening spiritually, I had many fears about what this meant. This was due to what I had been taught in life. After clearing my own harsh past life experiences, and current life traumas, and working through my fears from society's false conditioning and programming, I was able to open my heart, ready for the Divine messages that were waiting for me.

We will work on that in the next chapter and address what is in the shadows for you, so we may bring it out into the light and overcome what keeps you in fear.

18. If You Focus Too Hard to Get Details, Then Let Go of That, Take a Deep Breath, and Focus Lightly on Something Else.

The most amazing epiphanies come when you least expect them, and if you hyper-fixate on something, you may not have a clear answer or knowing because you are trying too hard. This is easy to forget. Keep this fun! If you are frustrated, then drop whatever you are doing, and either shift your mind to something else or drop what you are doing completely. Many times, I will feel like I hit a wall during a reading with someone, and they don't understand or resonate with something I've said. After many years of doing readings, I now know to just let it go for a while. When I shift perspective and go on to something else, my Guides pop in and blurt something out that explains what they were trying to relay to me differently. You can ask your Guides to give you the message in a different way! Sometimes this works for me, and sometimes it doesn't. At times, this is because the client sees things in a different way than Spirit is showing me. After a few more intuitive messages, it all makes sense.

19. Don't Be Surprised if Spirit Throws Your Client Under the Bus (So to Speak).

Sometimes, the Divine spirit wants to get a very serious message through that IS appropriate but feels like you are scolding them. This may be when that person needs to make better choices, and need a huge wake-up call, or a slap in the face. Spirit will use you to relay those messages. As a reader, this can be tough, but their Guides really want them to hear the messages they have given you. I have had this time and time again, and I will look to the Heavens and say to them in my mind, *"I DON'T want to tell them that!"* They stand in front of me with arms crossed and tell me they won't give me any more information UNTIL I relay the message. They are comical because they act as though they are bored and look away from me and pretend they are looking at their nails. When this happens, I ask them to give me this harsh information gently to relay to my client respectfully. The majority of the time, the client already knows, and they tell me they are well aware they need to make changes on the subject. Most times in my experience, I am just one of many messengers that have told them the same thing.

20. The Proof is in the Pudding! Don't Let Fear Stop You!

When you connect to the Divine and let your feelings and emotions take a back seat, you will channel such amazing and surprising information. The more you take yourself and your ego out of the picture, the easier this work is, and the information flows. Spirit has your back! Trust them to give you accurate information! They will prove to your client, or the recipient of a channeled message, that you are real. Don't focus on anything but that, and you will notice when you begin to talk, all kinds of things come out of your mouth. This feels like you are just chatting with a friend, and you have this flow of words that you say to them. Let it flow. This is Spirit channeling those Divine messages through you. They are sending a stream of information that you connect into and relay from them. Your Spirit Guides and the client's Spirit Guides are working together to send you a stream of conscious information that flows through you that is easily communicated to your client. Every day, I am amazed while doing this work and how things that come out of my mouth are very accurate details of someone's life experience that I had no clue of.

Can you think of all the times you were chatting with a friend and some advice popped out of your mouth for them? If it wasn't your mind thinking those thoughts prior, it was most definitely Spirit helping you and them!

Shadow Work

Chapter 6

Shadow Work, What Lurks in Your Shadows? Journey with Your Angels to Heal.

What is shadow work? It is the root reason for what may be weighing you down emotionally or physically. It is what lurks in the shadows of your subconscious mind, causing feelings of anxiety, fear, emotional pain, anger, and lower vibrational feelings.

When you are triggered by something in your life, or are really angry, or irritated for no apparent reason with someone or something, it could be the result of past traumas bubbling to the surface that need to be seen, worked through, and cleared.

Shadow work is needed to find what lies dormant inside yourself, in the shadows of your soul. Your soul has been through many lifetimes and experiences. Your soul may be bruised, shattered, beaten, and abused. Deep soul work is imperative to move forward on the path of enlightenment. When you dig deep and find out where your triggers and fears come from, you need to expose them, dig them up from the dirt, and find a way to heal them. Those experiences may be from previous lifetimes, this current lifetime, or even future lifetimes.

Each time you do this, you help yourself to ascend to a higher vibration. You feel lighter, more at ease, and get triggered less and less by situations. It is very much like a roller coaster. If you don't stop the train and let yourself move through and flow with the ups and downs of the roller coaster of emotions, your spiritual team will step in to assist you.

You have a spiritual team on the other side of the veil, and you have teachers and Helpers called light-workers or way-showers, such as me, that are here on Earth. I have been through many years of these experiences and now have agreed to step up and show others how to help themselves. When you ask for a teacher, they appear. I had many wonderful teachers on my path and continue to have them in my life.

How do you ask for help? Simply think it! Say it out loud or say it in your mind. By doing this, you send out energy into the world that goes to your spiritual team of Angels, Spirit Guides, and Divine ancestors to get your wishes started. They help us in so many ways!

This book is designed to help you on that path. You simply need to ask them for assistance and they get busy helping you behind the scenes. They can see through time and space (which really does not exist, it is all happening at once) and see possible outcomes for each decision with clarity. They give us information through our psychic centers to help us with the most soul growth. They are there for guidance when we, as humans, feel blind, deaf, and closed off from our true Divine state of being.

My Spirit Guides showed me in the likeness of Helen Keller and how her teacher had to find ways to help her to understand the outside world when she was in the dark. Her teacher was there to help guide her from that dark place where she didn't know how to communicate and felt lost, trapped, and alone.

To raise your vibration to speak with Spirit and Angels who have crossed to the light, you must clear the low emotions and fears to be able to climb that ladder of consciousness.

Anyone can channel spirits and beings. You channel spirits and beings at the level of consciousness that you are at yourself. That means if you are in a very angry or low place emotionally, you will attract spirits and entities that match that frequency.

Artists, painters, and writers often channel from different dimensions. They may also be remembering spiritual gifts they had from other lifetimes or from in between lifetimes where they had extraordinary talents and abilities.

Your vibration has a base that is set by your soul experiences (lessons learned) from all of your lifetimes. The more soul missions (lifetimes) you have experienced, learned from, and are considered complete, the more soul growth you have, which helps you to have your base at a higher level.

Close your eyes, take a deep breath, and see where your base is for your consciousness. Ask your team of light to give you messages or pictures in your mind to help you see where you are. You can also look at yourself and how you respond to things in your life as to where you are. Be honest. If you are not honest with yourself, this won't work. Imagine you are someone else who is seeing the real you, your skeletons and all.

~~~

Exercise

Ask some questions about yourself and note them in your journal.

1. What is your personality like? Are you sunny and full of sunshine or do you sulk? Do you have bitterness in your heart for others for no apparent reason?

2. How do you deal with contrast in life? Do you fly off the handle?

3. How do you treat others? Do you treat them with respect and dignity?

4. How do you treat yourself?

5. How do you treat the Earth, animals, and children?

6. Do you have skeletons in your closet? What do you ignore or push down that makes you feel ill, negative, or experience bad emotions?

7. If there is a pole for your level of consciousness, where would it be from 1 to 100?

8. Every human is here to figure these things out, know that you are NOT alone!

9. Ask yourself and your team to help you find ways of dialing that pole up. Ask them to help you find ways to be kinder to others, yourself, and the environment.

10. Ask them to help you find ways to find the root of why you respond in negative ways and ask them to help you on your path to clear roadblocks that are stopping you on your Divine path to the light!

11. Are you ready to let go of old, stagnated energy? How do you see it holding you back in your life? Do you push people away because of it?

I see this as a garden that is within each one of us on Earth. We need to keep tending our gardens so they don't rot, get overgrown with weeds, and out of control. Daily, we must tend to our gardens by showing up and doing the work. The following is a guided meditation/journey to help you dig in and find your rotten roots, pull them from the root, and heal them. This is connected to your Akashic records, which are the records from all your lifetimes and holds the key to opening those previously closed spiritual doors.

Please note, when doing this deeply spiritual work, you will be shown what needs to be cleared with grace and love by your spiritual team of light and Angels. Relax. Know you are safe and well cared for and surrounded by your loving soul family.

~~~

Exercise

Meditation to Clear the Decaying Roots in Your Spiritual Garden – Clearing the Shadows

1. Take a deep breath in, allowing your spiritual channels called chakras to spin clockwise from head to toe. Intend that this is Divine sparkling light from the Heaven's that is raining into your body. Breathe that delicious loving light into every cell of your body, flowing it through each energy center of your body and into the Earth.

2. Now expand that energy to your entire auric field around you. You control your auric field. Now you are filled within your physical body and have circled your body with this amazing light from the Heavens.

3. Your breath brings that flowing shower of energy into every cell. What color – or colors – does this energy look like? Does it look like raindrops of light? It is high vibrational crystalline light and clearing energy that is always flowing to you if you allow it.

4. Let your intuition guide you to bring through the color of the light.

5. Ask your team of light and Archangels to come and assist you. Ask them to help you find your shadows and pull them up for you to heal. Feel yourself feel surrounded as a soft loving feeling

comes through your body, letting you know you are safe and surrounded by Angel wings.

6. Ask your Angels to sweep your auric field clean of any heavy feelings or emotions that have settled into your energy field. Ask your Angels to help clear the space around you.

7. Allow yourself to be lifted by these Angel wings that surround you. They hold you in love, lifting you easily and softly. Take a breath in and allow yourself to be lifted. Feel your light body lift, feeling full of heavenly weightlessness. You will stay floating on this soft bed of Angel wings until it's time to come back. You are safe, and they will help you in the softest way possible.

8. Allow the Angels to beam light into your body and drift off into a lovely state of light consciousness where you are in a light dream-like state.

9. You have now moved into a room of white light, and you are in this lovely soft bed of large Angel feathers. You have a beautiful large-screen television in front of you. You have the remote control, and you are going to watch from a distance the scenes that your Guides and Angels have prepared for you.

10. You have the remote in your hand and can pause, stop, rewind, or fast-forward the movie as you choose. You have control.

11. Ask your Angels to show you your movie. This movie may be from another lifetime or this current lifetime. Allow them to show you what is the root of an emotional response you experience in your life. Ask them to be gentle and show you what you need to know without trauma. If you don't see with your mind's eye, ask them to give you the information in the way of knowing, feeling, hearing, or sensing.

12. Push play. Allow the scene to play out. Remember, you have asked for the cliff notes version which cuts out any traumatic scenes. If you choose to see the experience in its entirety, then that is your choice.

13. Notice the way you feel and allow those feelings and emotions to come up. Call on your Angels to help you see, feel, or know what you need to know from that experience.

14. Ask your Angels to assist you in finding the best way to either rewrite this experience or to clear it. You may choose to just let it go, knowing what caused your pain and releasing it.

15. Rewrite your story or timeline. Ask your Angels to assist you in rewinding the scene to a point before the trauma happened. This is especially important for extreme traumas so it clears them from your soul memory. Rewind to a point where that aspect of yourself feels happier and change the story to a different ending that helps you. You may choose to change a simple decision, which then changes the story line, thereby not putting you in a bad situation. You may decide to be kinder to someone or heal a feud that led to their original fate of doom.

16. If that aspect of you is supposed to pass and you don't want to change it, you can ask the Angels, Jesus, Mother Mary, or any Ascended Master to assist them by lifting them out of the body before the bad experience happens and surround them with Angels and Guides to remove them from the trauma completely.

17. When they are lifted out of the body, they no longer experience the painful death and are held in light by the Angels until the physical body expires and releases the cord that attaches the light body to the physical body. That cord releases from the physical

body and then they ascend into the Heavens and the golden light of Source. This is crossing the pearly gates, and they go home.

18. Say goodbye to this aspect of yourself as it goes. Most often, they will give a gift of a piece of light that belongs to you. It may look like a puzzle piece or a token as a gift they give to you. This represents a piece of your soul that was trapped in that time and space and is now glowing with light. Accept this as a piece of your soul coming back to you that is cleared, cleansed, and whole. Breathe it into your light body and feel or see it go back to where it belongs within you.

19. This is a gift of appreciation, but also calling a piece of your soul back to you, otherwise known as soul retrieval.

20. Feel that aspect ascend into the golden light and feel that spiritual doorway close after they go through it.

21. You have completed your mission. Thank your Angels and leave the room of light as a beautiful tube of light appears to float you home. Allow yourself to go into that tunnel of light and fly through amazing multicolored light energies that cleanse you on the journey back to your physical body.

22. Feel yourself float back into your body. Take a deep breath in and set the intention that you are anchored into your physical body, grounded, centered, and full of Divine light.

23. Notice where that piece of soul settled back into your light body.

24. Your old root has been dug up, released, and cleansed.

25. Ask yourself what your inner garden looked like before this journey, and what does it look like or feel like now?

26. You may repeat this journey as many times as you feel is necessary.

27. Ground your roots back into Mother Earth and give thanks to all your helpers for their love and assistance.

Shadow work comes up in layers when you are ready to experience it, release it, and heal it. If you can't do this work on your own, find someone to assist you. Sometimes we need others that have that knowledge and experience to help us dig up our roots, and to tend our gardens. Be gentle with yourself. This work takes time, and you will face your deepest fears and go through those experiences to learn and heal.

This meditation is a combination of teachings that I received from Yeshua, and he showed me that is how he did his healing while on Earth. There is no need to go into deep trauma and relive that experience. Some people need to go through each step and know everything that happened to them. For others, it's not necessary. This method is a combination of hypnosis, spirit travel/journey, Akashic journey, and shamanic soul retrieval. This helps you to release harsh experiences and call back your power. There are many other ways of doing that work and I recommend you try many modalities. Sound healing, including the expression of anger and emotional issues, is needed many times. Don't hold emotions in because it blocks the energy field. EFT Tapping is another wonderful way of releasing, hypnotherapy, and many others.

Chapter 7

THE CONSCIOUS AND SUBCONSCIOUS MIND

Chapter 7

The Conscious and Subconscious Mind Explained, and Levels of Brainwave Stages A Guidebook to Awaken Your Divine Psychic Abilities

In the last chapter, I spoke about different levels of consciousness. This will be a quick explanation of the four parts of the conscious mind.

The four parts of the conscious mind are rational, analytical, willpower, and temporary memory.

The conscious mind is where we are most of our awake time. The conscious mind is the rational and analytical part of the mind. This is the state where we do our thinking and judging. I would call this 3D thinking. It is what is in front of you and what may feel like a logical thought, or what you see is what is your reality. The rational mind isn't always correct and it will always try to create a way to find a solution or reason for experiences.

Willpower is part of the conscious mind. This is what drives you, but it also provides short bursts of energy to get through a situation.

Temporary memory is what we use in daily life to help us along in our lives such as remembering people, names, places, and experiences. Our conscious mind can only hold small amounts of information at one time.

The subconscious mind uses imagination, permanent memory, habits, feelings of emotions, beliefs, and the autonomic nervous system.

The subconscious mind is the most powerful part of our mind. This is the part that is in control and where imagination is accessed. Your subconscious mind houses your permanent memories, and when you want to go back through time and space to relive your experiences, this is where you come as these experiences comprise your permanent memories. Our subconscious mind allows us to feel emotions and experiences that we cannot feel when we are in the 3D (conscious) state of mind. Our permanent memory is where information is stored, much like a computer database, and you can tap into this database with deep soul work. Deep soul work includes a spirit journey, meditation, zoning out, hypnosis, and sound healing. This work and the state that you achieve allows you to let yourself go into various states of relaxation, and by being relaxed, these memories may bubble up to the surface.

Habits, feelings, beliefs, and emotions are also in the subconscious mind. When you begin to tap into these relaxed and safe places within your subconscious mind, you can tap into these feelings, beliefs, habits, and emotions. You can find reasons for WHY you react to situations, or how your conscious mind works. This is all connected to your personality, how you relate to the world, and how you may feel in positive or negative situations.

Our autonomic nervous system drives what we do automatically such as eating, breathing, beating our heart, and flowing our blood. This part of the subconscious mind helps us to live, and I am told by my guides, that it is intertwined with our DNA. It is hardwired into us so that we can continue to grow and expand as a species.

I am told by Spirit that we are expanding and upgrading our autonomic nervous systems by spiritually awakening and lifting to higher levels of vibration. Animals are born with more automatic *knowings* of how to do things, automatically knowing what is not safe, such as naturally averting fire or avoiding ingestion of a plant or food that may kill or make them ill. As a human race, we will continue to have these extraordinary senses sharpened as we rise in consciousness. New generations being born will continue to walk sooner, develop a stronger sense of danger, recall their previous lifetimes, and much more. According to my guides, this is all due to the rising consciousness on Earth.

Next, there are different levels of relaxation for sleep that may help you to understand the different stages of meditative states that I mentioned earlier.

The three levels of relaxation/sleep stages, also known as brainwave stages, are:

Alpha: As the physical body starts to relax, alpha brainwaves begin. This is a light meditative state and is relaxing. This is where you may zone out. For me, I shift into a state of mind where I am floating away in my mind and focusing on what is coming into my mind. I can still sense things around me happening, but it goes into the background. I go into a deep thought state. The best way to describe this state is like I am daydreaming.

This is the KEY to downloading Divine messages and information. If you are relaxed, this is where you download messages and information to help you on your path. You can learn to *will* yourself into this light meditative state by thinking about it, taking a breath, and releasing all thoughts and feelings. You may feel light and bubbly like you are rising, feeling full of happy and light energy. When you attain this light state, you allow yourself to meet your Spirit Guides and Helpers in the middle. They come down to assist you.

This state of mind happens all the time during your waking state. It may happen while driving, working out, doing a repetitive job, or even relaxing. Can you relate to experiences like when you are driving and you realize you don't remember how you got there? Or driving through traffic lights without consciously seeing them? Or when you went into an automatic mode? It can be a bit frightening when you realize this. Who is driving the car during this time? It feels like you went into autopilot while you downloaded information.

Theta: This is the brainwave stage of brain activity where the physical body shuts down from experiencing most sensations. Awareness disconnects from the physical body so it can focus on the astral or light body. This state of being can be achieved through deep meditation or relaxation.

Delta: This is the stage where complete awareness is lost and typically lasts for around 30 minutes. It takes deep work to reach this stage and complete loss of reality from the 3D world. This is also known as a state of hypnosis and this is where you can astral project from your physical body. We reach all three stages of brainwaves each night during sleep and move back and forth between them. This is where you reach the dream state and access your subconscious memories.

According to my Spirit Guides, this is where our Higher Selves come in to assist and help us to clear out what hides in our shadows.

Chapter 8

Spiritual Dimensions

Chapter 8

Spiritual Dimensions, How Your Chakras Connect to Layers of the Aura, and the Three Worlds of Shamanism

Spiritual dimensions differ from the conscious, subconscious, and brainwave levels. There are rings of energy within our auric field around our bodies that connect with our main chakras starting from the crown chakra to the root chakra (from the head to the bottom). These connect the energy centers within our light bodies to the outer rings of energy around our bodies. This is how they correlate beginning with the crown (the top of the head).

This explains why there are many colored layers when you energetically look in the auric field. The person's emotions and feelings shift the colors of the auric field. This looks to me like a jawbreaker candy that has been cut in half with a rainbow of colors inside.

The Seven-Layer Auric Body System Correlation to Main Chakras

On the spiritual plane, our seven-layer auric body system and main chakras connect us to the Divine or the Ether:

Crown chakra – etheric body (mental aspect) *Ether, the state between energy and matter. This ring of energy is furthest away from the body.

Third eye chakra – celestial body (emotional aspect) *Associated with feelings and follows the outline of the physical body. This ring of energy is 6 away from the body.

Throat chakra – etheric template (physical aspect). This ring of energy is 5 away from the body.

On the astral plane/bridge/in-between the ether and physical 3D world:

Heart chakra – astral body. This ring of energy is 4 away from the body.

On the physical plane within the physical 3D world:

Solar plexus – mental body (lower mental aspect). This ring of energy is 3 away from the body.

Sacral chakra – emotional body (lower emotional aspect). This ring of energy is 2 away from the body.

Root chakra – etheric body (lower etheric aspect). This ring of energy is the closest to the body.

Another way to describe energetic dimensions is through the three worlds in shamanism.

There are three worlds, and these consist of:

The upper world (Heaven).
The middle world (the 3D world where we are now and in the now).
The lower world (under the Earth).

There are many dimensions within all three of these worlds. Please note that this is how I experienced these dimensions, and you and others, may see these in different ways. That does not mean it isn't correct. It simply means this is the way my spirit team showed me. If you go on spirit journeys such as this, make sure you are asking your Angels and Guides to keep you clear of negative energies and entities. I ask them to assist me, come with me, and I travel in a tube of Divine white light.

I see it in my mind's eye as bands of color that you can move through, resembling bands of sound waves that you can travel through. The dimensions are everywhere, but for me to be able to understand them, I asked my Guides to take me on a journey to show me what they mean. On a shamanic journey to the upper world, I was taken up to the heavenly realm and shown the different dimensions. I knew the dimensions weren't like a ladder or staircase, but for me to understand, I asked them to show me them in this fashion.

The dimensions are at different frequencies of energy, much like the poles of polarity.

On my journey, I went up through the lower frequency dimensions of what we call purgatory. I see these dimensions as heavier, darker places that are not fun places to be. Each human has the option of crossing over to the light when they pass, and for many reasons, some choose not to. I will cover that in the chapter on crossing over spirits.

As I went up to the heavens, I saw these as darker dimensions. As I went up higher, they got lighter. There are many shades and levels of the purgatory dimensions.

I kept moving up and above the light gray dimension, and I saw the pearly gates. There was a Gatekeeper that allowed me and my Guides to enter. This is real folks! When you cross those gates, you feel the light of Source flows through you. It feels like home. I went through and saw a blinding white light, and then saw my family members. They were having a dinner party and welcoming me. My Guides took me up from there to dimensions that went higher and higher. The next dimension took me to my Spirit Guide dimension, then on to the Ascended Master dimension, then to the Angels, Archangels, and Source. There are unlimited dimensions and many in between these. I haven't started to scratch the surface to understand how many there are. They also showed me that the dimensions aren't only in heaven, but they exist everywhere since there is no time or space.

This explains how my mother can stand next to me and tell me she is just a dimension away, and there is just a thin veil between us.

I have also been shown during readings and spiritual work that the dimensions are much like bands of light within the etheric realm that you can move through with your light body, much like jumping on a cloud, to different frequencies of energy and color. I see this as a psychedelic world of color and beams of light you can travel around in.

There are many dimensions with lower vibrational entities and lower dimensions. I would not recommend doing this spiritual travel if you are not guided by a teacher, or on a guided spiritual journey.

The lower world is much different than the upper world in my experience. It is much like *Alice in Wonderland*. It is mystical, magical, and so much fun to explore. You can meet spirit animals and helpers there as well.

Inter-dimensional beings exist. Fairies, gnomes, elves, and many others exist within Earthly dimensions and have been here since the beginning of Earth. They can be positive, but some might not be. If you are respectful to the Earth, you should not have many problems with them. I would recommend learning about them before you work with them. The fairy folk has been seen and felt by intuitive people since time began. They are here to keep the Earth clean and help with farming, pollination, water, plants, and flowers. If you are respectful of them, they will be respectful of you. The dimension they reside in is not far from ours.

I see them in my yard when I am quiet. I see them in my mind's eye. I feel them like fluttering energy, they are thankful for me and the work I do to help heal the Earth and they bring a high vibration.

The fairy folk has been raising their vibration along with us. They are similar to Angels but are within the Earthly realm to do Divine work here.

How do you perceive the different dimensions?

I have just explained how I see them. Every individual has different filters and ways of thinking that cast a unique-to-them perspective of other realms. It is important to do meditations and spirit work for you to have your own unique experiences within other dimensional realms. This work is sacred and fun! It is also extremely important that you do this work with assistance from your Angels and Guides. They help you stay safe.

I had experiences where I didn't realize that I should ask them to assist me while spiritually traveling through these realms. I picked up negative spiritual attachments. If you simply ask your team of light to come with you and help you to stay safe, they will guide you within realms of Divine light. I call it a tube of light that I travel through, and it keeps anything that isn't of the light from being able to reach me.

Keeping yourself clean and clear is very important. Ensure you clear your light body before and after any spiritual practice. Then ground your energy back to Earth so you are in balance. Please refer to Chapter 2 of this book which explains how to clear your energy field. After you get the hang of it, you can clear your light body in a very short period of time!

~~~

Exercise

Meditative Exercise to See into Other Dimensions

1. Get comfortable, relax, and lay down or sit comfortably in your sacred space. Make sure you are alone and won't have an outside influence of any kind, including animals, children, phone calls, or anything that takes you from a deep meditation.

2. Ask your spiritual team to guide you on this spiritual journey. Ask them to keep you safe and guide you to see or feel the universe and its dimensions. Set any intentions you may have for this journey.

3. Envision a beautiful shower of Divine rainbow light flowing down from the heavens, engulfing you in a spectacular show of flashing and pulsating light energy that permeates your entire being, inside and out. It flows through each chakra and every cell of your body. It flows out to each layer of your auric field and sizzles through it, cleansing and clearing all forms of harsh thoughts and emotions that you have held within your light body. Allow it to dissolve in this multicolored electric light show within you.

4. Ask your team of light to take your etheric hand and take you on a journey. Take a deep breath in, and on the exhale, allow yourself to lift up and out of the 3D world, and into an open door of light that is in front of you. Notice the details of this door of light. Is the door round or does it look like a door with a knob? Allow your team of light to pull you into this door and through it.

5. Allow yourself to be drawn into this Divine tunnel of sparkling, crystalline light. Notice the colors as you float forward. Feel the energy. Allow yourself to flow weightlessly in the Divine flow as it pulls you forward. You can swim in this flow of energy. You can do somersaults. Have fun in this space. This is where you travel each night in your dreams. Allow your Guides to take you to different places. If you don't visualize, then feel the energy pulling you in different directions. Allow whatever may come in.

6. As you do this journey, are visions popping up? Do you see colors or animals? What do these dimensions look like? Do you feel like you are traveling in space and into the stars and planets? Allow yourself to be taken where you've never traveled before. Feel the movement, sense the energy shifting from one dimension to another. You may travel in many directions. Do you have any smells that come in? Do you hear your Angels laughing or singing?

7. Can you see into the dimensions that I spoke about? If you were to allow your team of light to show you, what would these dimensions look like to you? Take your time. You are safe and in the hands of the beings of light that have been helping you all your life. Allow them to show you into a room that was created just for you. As you come into this room, what is in here? Do you feel light, and weightless? Can you jump up and down or fly with just a thought? Put your arms out and fly. There is no gravity here, and the breath combined with your thoughts propel you in any direction. Fly up above the trees. Anywhere your heart desires. Notice this beautiful place of Divine love and what it looks like to you. Take as much time here as you'd like.

8. When you are done with this journey, allow your guides to take your hand again. Right in front of you, another door of light

magically opens. Fly into this Divine tube of light and allow it to bring you back to your body.

9. The tube of light brings you back, glittering with light, and throughout your body, you feel a wonderful buzzing energy. Call your energy back to your body. Settle back into your physical body. Thank your team of light for a wonderful journey.

10. Ground your energy and come back to a waking state. Rest and reflect on what you just experienced and drink a glass of water. Journal all your experiences.

Chapter 9

DIVINATION TOOLS

A guide to using Oracle, Tarot, Angel Cards, and The Pendulum

Chapter 9

Your Spiritual Toolbox! Divination Tools and How They Help You Open Up Spiritually

Divination tools are very helpful and they help you to create your spiritual toolbox. The definition of divination from Merriam-Webster's dictionary is:

Divination-noun; div·i·na·tion, ˌdi-və-ˈnā-shən 1: the art or practice that seeks to foresee or foretell future events or discover hidden knowledge usually by the interpretation of omens or by the aid of supernatural powers 2: unusual insight: intuitive perception. (Merriam-Webster n.d.)

Some Different forms of divination include:

Tarot cards
Oracle cards
Angel cards
Runes
I-Ching (coins)
Numerology
Automatic writing
Animal messages
Tea leaves (reading)
Palmistry
Dowsing Rods (L-shaped rods)
Pendulum (dowsing)

Scrying (letting your eyes defocus and getting images)

Crystal reading

Dice

Playing cards

Candle flame

Book

Smoke signals

Mirror

Ouija board (Not recommended without substantial training)

Divination tools are keys that help you unlock your locked spiritual doors. They give you messages and knowledge that allow you to take the focus off yourself and your ego. They give you guidance and direction that help you open spiritual doors and step through to greater wisdom and knowledge that is awaiting you. They show you where to begin during a psychic reading and help you pick up intuitive messages. It paints a picture for you to view and then goes on to form a story. This is how psychic reading comes, flowing in freely. You are the channel for the Divine messages that are flowing through and to you. Divination tools allow you to focus on them instead of yourself (and the feeling of what you may or not be doing correctly) and allow you to receive Divine light energy without the chatter of your mind.

I will focus on oracle cards and the pendulum, giving you my guidance to work with these divinatory tools. If you already practice with tarot cards, or other tools, my guidance applies to all of them.

These tools open spiritual doorways to other dimensions, connecting you to your team of guides; however, if you don't set intentions and specify what it is you expect, you will call in all kinds of things that are out there in the Universe. This is NOT what you want.

I will state some safety measures to help you have a wonderful and enlightening experience with your divination tools.

Please do these next steps on intuition alone. This is a way to practice your intuitive messages. Try not to look or refer to the guidebook that comes with your cards. Don't look anything up on the internet for meaning. This is how you can sharpen your intuition. Allow your spiritual team to give you all that you need.

Guidebooks can be helpful for you when you do readings, but for now, try without them. You will get lovely messages that may differ from what the books say. That does NOT mean that the information is incorrect. It simply means that you received different messages than what was written in the guidebook. When doing this with a group, all of you will receive similar messages and Spirit will connect it all. Spirit is showing you the whole story.

Before my spiritual awakening and learning how psychic things work, I believed that there was one answer to a question and that everyone who is psychic, should get the same message. WRONG. You can be in a group of twenty people, and every single person may get a different message. They are all given different pieces of a larger puzzle. So, they are all working as a team to put the puzzle together! If you ask a yes or no question, almost all the answers will match, but details received on the same question can go in many directions. Recently, I taught a class on this subject while I writing this book! This happened time and time again. We were unanimous in answers regarding yes or no questions, but the details for each yes or no answer brought up different topics and subtopics. With each of these came guidance. Spirit is so amazing with how they have us working as a team!

Not looking up answers in the books makes it much more fun, and it shows you how intuitive you are! No cheating!

~~~

Exercise

How to Draw Oracle and Tarot Cards Based on Intuition.

(You can read the books that come along with oracle or tarot cards and use their methods, but first, try to do it intuitively without a specific way).

(Steps 1 – 4 apply for all divination tools):

1. Call on those who ONLY walk in the white light and have the most Divine love for you and humanity. Nothing else is allowed in your Divine space. Not knowing this gem of a tool can get you into hot water.

2. Clear yourself, your space, and the tools you are using. Flow the Divine light in from above and below, and send that light through you, and out of your hands and heart, filling them with Divine love and light. It flows with your breath. Envision this light filling your spiritual tool. This is when you set the intention with your Angels and Spirit Guides, asking for Divine direction, messages, and answers to your question. Raise your spiritual antennae for them to connect with you. Raise your vibration to one hundred percent.

Please note: if you are using oracle cards, tarot cards, cards, or a book, you can lightly tap the deck or book. This knocks the old energy from the cards or the book. Then, fill and flood it with Divine light. If you can, use your mind's eye to watch this happen. Feel the energy enter your light body, and with your breath, fill the object with sparkling light. I learned this and many more wonderful tips from my amazing teacher and mentor, Bonnie Burd. Thank you, Bonnie! Love you!

3. Ask simple questions one at a time. Your spiritual team needs to know what you want to inquire about. Be specific with what you are asking about. You may also just leave it open for whatever Spirit wants you to know.

4. After filling your tool with light, and setting intentions, draw your cards.

5. Prior to pulling cards, clear your deck. Then, go through your deck and look at each one. Pay attention to the pictures, numbers, and words on each card. This will help you become familiar with your deck.

Ask for guidance on how many cards to draw. You may receive a number in your mind, you may hear it, or have a number pop up. If you are using cards, shuffle them, and think about your question.

6. Draw cards intuitively as you shuffle the deck. Some cards may pop out unexpectedly and some might even fly out. You will have a feeling if you should or should not use that card. Go with your first instinct. I shuffle the cards and the ones that pop up in the deck or that draw me to them, are the ones I choose. If you feel inclined, fan the cards out on a table. You can run your hand over them slowly and use your sense of touch to draw you to a card. You can also allow your eyes to be drawn to a card.

7. Choose as many cards as you feel appropriate. Put them in front of you from left to right. They read like a book, from left to right. When a card is upside down, it normally means the opposite of the message.

Pay attention to the numbers, pictures, and feelings of the card. Pick up the first card. Feel the energy of it. Be open to any messages that may come through. Focus on the pictures and allow the information to easily flow in. Flow it in with your breath, through your spiritual antennae.

8. Allow the messages to come in with each card. Can you see a flow of information that reads like a story in the cards? What comes to mind when you look at the pictures? Defocus your eyes when you look at the cards and see what appears in your mind's eye for you. Remember that you can receive psychic information in many different ways. You may also have phrases or words on the cards. They hold meaning, and that meaning may vary for you. What comes to mind? This is your intuition working. Allow it to flow!

9. Does the flow of information you are receiving paint a picture or create a story in your head? Do you have a sudden epiphany or instant knowing of something?

10. Thank your spirit helpers and ground your energy.

11. Next time, ask someone you know if you can practice reading for them. Remember, they have to be willing to participate.

Numbers Have Meaning! Basic Numerology Meanings From 1 – 9:

1 – action, new beginnings, the start of a cycle

2 – love, relationships, sensitivity

3 – joy, light, socialness, communication, expression

4 – hard work, organization, structure, security

5 – change, transformation, travel, adventure

6 – family, service, compassion, duty

7 – spiritual development, reflection time, quietude, retreat

8 – money, power, success

9 – karma, releasing, completions, end of a cycle or chapter

Numbers are also amazing messages in themselves. They are also known as angel numbers. They have more meaning when numbers are repeated. Notice with oracle, tarot, or angel cards, they may have a number listed on them.

For instance, the number 1 means action, new beginnings, and the start of a cycle.

The number 11 is often referred to as the "inner teacher". You spend so much of your time looking out and comparing yourself to others, but this angel number is a reminder that you should spend more time looking toward yourself. It's high time for you to bring your hidden skills to the surface.

Angel number 111 signifies the manifestation of wealth and prosperity. It's a strong number that relates to the possibility of your thoughts becoming your reality. The number '1' in 111 is a dominating number, which has many meanings. The '1' symbolizes confidence, awareness, independence, uniqueness, sureness, and motivation.

You can look these numbers up on the internet or buy a book on numerology or angel numbers that explains these in greater detail.

The Pendulum

The pendulum is commonly thought of as a pointed crystal attached to a string or chain. Holding the chain or string with your hands, the pendulum moves with energy in response to questions. The pendulum is a physical object but is a spiritual tool that can be made of wood, metal, crystal, or any natural object that speaks to you. Any item can be used as a pendulum, and often, I have removed my necklace and used it as a pendulum. One of the most common uses of a pendulum, and the most known, is to determine the gender of a baby for a pregnant woman and her partner.

What Can You Do with a Pendulum?

*Ask questions to your spiritual team.

*Find spiritual portals.

*Clear energy from places or people.

*Chakra energy clearing is a wonderful way of using your pendulum.

*You can ask your spiritual team to assist you in finding things. It may pull in a specific direction to show you something you can't find, much like divining (or dowsing) rods. Divining rods are L-shaped rods that are held in both hands and help you find water sources or metals in the Earth.

*You can use a pendulum for most anything you can think of!

~~~

Exercise

How to Use Your Pendulum: FIRST Clear Space and Your Pendulum

1. Pick your pendulum, or better yet, let it pick you! Crystals, rocks, gems, and spiritual tools must feel like a spiritual fit for you.

You will be drawn to it, and you may feel like it speaks to you. When I work with my pendulums, they almost seem to dance with energy. They may even sway or move on their own when you are next to them in a store. Most often, I spiritually hear it speak to me, telling me to take it home, and that it wants to work with me. Please note, some spiritual tools may be a fit for you for a time, but then you will be guided to give them to someone else that needs them later. If this is the case, then please know that your time with it has finished and it is now meant for someone else. I have had this happen many times, even when I just purchased a beautiful crystal. One that came to mind was when I went to a dear friend's home a few weeks after I bought a beautiful and rare opal crystal. I heard, in my mind, *"Give it to her!"* I thought, what a bummer, I really like this one! I heard it again to give it to her. It wasn't mine. I gave her the opal crystal, and then soon after, I received another one. She needed it for her home. It wasn't meant for me anymore. I have had this with many of my spiritual tools including my first pendulum, many crystals, and even a unicorn oracle deck.

2. Clear your space and the pendulum, set your intentions, and raise your vibration.

You will also want to clear the energy in your pendulum. To clear this spiritual tool, simply envision filling it with light, from your hands and your whole body. If you feel the object is full of Divine light, then proceed. If not, then use another method of cleansing it. If it is made of crystal, you can run it under running water, set it in the sun (to clear it), and in the moonlight (to charge it). You can put it in salt for some time. If you don't feel a good and loving high vibration to this spiritual tool, then it may not be for you! Use your gut instinct and pay attention to how it feels to you. If you have just bought your pendulum, any crystals, or any spiritual tools such as oracle cards from a store, then you will want to cleanse the energy from them and infuse your energy signature of light and love into it. If you think about it, how many other people touched those objects? When you realize that their energies are also infused into that object, you will want it to be cleansed so it will be energetically in harmony with you and only you. One exception to this is when you do a harmonious ceremony and put your crystals in the center of the room and charge it with your light infused with others, then the energy can become multiplied with Divine light. This would be an example of how and when other people's high vibrational energy, combined with yours, help to enhance the vibratory energy of that crystal.

If a pendulum or spiritual tool doesn't appear to give you the best information, or simply won't work well for you, then it may not be meant for you. Take this as a sign and see if another one works better for you.

3. Using your pendulum.

After filling your pendulum with light, and setting the intention of love, light, and only Divine loving guidance, it's time to ask your question. Your Higher Self and spiritual team of Guides and Angels are the ones helping you with the question you have, or what you have asked for help with. Please remember that they are not puppets trying to put on a show, but serious Divine spiritual helpers.

*Ask your Guides to help you learn to work with your pendulum. YOU decide what Yes and No mean by the way the pendulum swings. Set that intention. For example, let them know that back and forth means yes, and side to side means NO. You will ask very simple but specific yes and no questions. These must be specific so as not to be confusing.

*Hold your pendulum with your dominant hand at the end of the rope, string, or chain. Clear your mind.

*Practice with them asking them questions you know are right, like *"Is my name, Kathleen?"*

The more relaxed you are, the more the pendulum will swing. If you are not comfortable with the pendulum, it may not sway much. The more you work with your pendulum, the more it will work.

4. Important note: if you ask a question of the pendulum that you have strong feelings about, then your answer from it may not be accurate. Your feelings and emotions can make the pendulum move, and I would consider that a form of telekinesis.

According to the Merriam-Webster dictionary, telekinesis, te-li-kə-ˈnē-səs means:

> *the production of motion in objects (as by a spiritualistic medium) without contact or other physical means. In my words, you are moving things with your mind. (Merriam-Webster n.d.)*

If you are going to ask a question that you have emotional ties to, then ask someone else that you know (if they don't have feelings pertaining to the subject) to use this divining tool for you so the answer is genuine and not biased.

I have used pendulums for years, mostly for doing energy and chakra-clearing work. I have used the pendulum to answer yes and no questions, but not for very long and not often. Early in my spiritual learning, my Spirit Guides told me to ask them questions directly since I am clairaudient. I can hear my Spirit Guides in much more detail than a simple yes or no question.

The pendulum is a wonderful tool to use and can help you open up spiritually but it is a beginner's tool to help you to open up spiritually. When you feel blocked and can't hear your spiritual team, then it may help you unblock and hear.

Using the Pendulum to Clear Your Own Energy Body (Chakras)

Now that you know how to properly open up the sacred space to use your pendulum, I will talk about a few ways that you can use it to clear space and your own energy field of energy blockages.

Simple energy clearing with your pendulum.

Healthy Divine energy runs clockwise through your body. You can use a pendulum to clear blocked, stuck, or stagnant energy from your chakras (energy centers). I love to teach people to use a pendulum to clear energy blocks for themselves since they don't need to psychically see or feel the energy. The pendulum guides you and shows you what needs to be done.

There are two simple steps to clear your chakras with a pendulum:

1. Counter-clockwise rotation of the pendulum (left to right shoulder) in a circle will break up, pull out and dismantle blocked or heavy dense energy from the light body. I suggest that you sit up and use the pendulum with one hand holding it while the other lies palm up under it. After setting your intention, you can work on each chakra at a time, focusing on the 7 main chakras of the energy filed that go from the crown chakra down through the root chakra. Ask your guides and Angels to assist you. Allow the pendulum to begin swinging in a counterclockwise rotation. You can have the pendulum physically over a chakra in your body, or you can intend that the energy goes to a specific chakra. For example, to work on your crown chakra on top of your head, you can simply hold the pendulum with your dominant hand and hold your other hand open with the palm upwards and below the pendulum. Set the intention that the pendulum is clearing the energy within your crown chakra. Take a deep breath in and as you exhale, release all blocked, trapped, heavy energy, and emotions up and out of your crown. Feel it release with the breath (if possible). You may feel a pop of energy release, or you may feel lighter and relieved. You may see gray smoke energy leave your head in your mind's eye.

Do this until you feel you have let go of any dense energy from the crown chakra. When you are complete with the release of energy, the pendulum should stop spinning counterclockwise.

You have now released energy that was trapped in your crown chakra. Great job! This is only the first step.

In my mind's eye, I see a tornado of gray-to-black energy lifting from the chakra.

2. Fill in with Divine light from above and fill in your energy body with clockwise Divine light from the Source.

When the pendulum has completely stopped, it will reverse the direction and begin to spin down from the heavens spiraling in a clockwise (right to left shoulder) manner. Now, you are allowing in a shower of Divine light energy from the Heavens that comes down into your crown and fills it with light. Breathe in that Divine light and allow it to fill all the spaces that were just vacated by the heavier energy.

Set the intention that the Divine light fills the empty spaces in your crown chakra with the most Divine, sparkling crystalline light and swirls around, making your head feel light and floaty with a buzzing feeling of happiness.

You are done when the pendulum stops spinning clockwise and you feel like your head is in the clouds.

3. The crown is clear, now do the rest! Go through each main chakra to clear, cleanse, and fill with crystalline light. You may go crown to root chakra or do the opposite and go root to crown. You may also work on any part of your energy body such as a knee, ankle, or aura around your body. Whatever you choose is what is right for you!

If you have had a new injury or an old chronic physical ailment, then you can do this same process! Just set the intention that you are breaking up the old energy like a tornado breaking up the blocked energy that has been there, and dissolving it into a million pieces, transmuting it into the heavens.

4. When performing this type of chakra clearing, you may get visions, instant knowings, or aha- moments of what you are

releasing. Or you may not get anything! This is the beauty of pendulum clearing. It is doing the work with you and for you, but shows you proof that something is happening even if you can't intuitively see or feel it.

Clear Your Space, Home, or Business with the Same Technique!

You can clear your space, home, or business by doing the exact technique you used to clear your own energy body.

Set your intention to clear heavy or dense energy. Call in your Spiritual Guides and Angels. Ask Archangel Michael to assist in clearing your space.

*Counterclockwise rotation of the pendulum (left to right shoulder) in a circle will break up, pull out, and dismantle blocked or heavy dense energy from the room or space. Lift the energy into the Heavens and it will be transmuted into light.

*When the pendulum has completely stopped, it will reverse the direction and begin to spin down from the heavens, spiraling in a clockwise (right to left shoulder) manner. Now, you are allowing in a shower of Divine light energy from the Heavens, filling your room, home, and property with Divine light.

Extrasensory Perception & Psychometry

Chapter 10

Extrasensory Perception and Psychometry

According to Merriam Webster dictionary, psychometry is a noun, pronounced *psy·chom·e·try; sī- ˈkä-mə-trē*, and means:

> *divination of facts concerning an object or its owner through contact with or proximity to the object. (Merriam-Webster n.d.)*

It also states psychometry –

> *The ability to obtain information about a person or an object by touch. (Merriam-Webster n.d.)*

My definition of psychometry is the same! When you have an object that belonged to someone else, you may be able to hold it in your hand or touch it and receive psychic information from it. These abilities can be connected to objects, places, or people!

You may get psychic images, an instant knowing, or you may hear a spirit speak to you! This is a wonderful way to practice your spiritual skills! Use your intuition if that object has an energetically good feeling. If you sense negativity, then don't use that object. As you move on in your spiritual journey, you may get more and more spiritually sensitive to energies. I noticed that I began to get an overwhelming feeling when I walked into a store with antiques. Sometimes, negative energy gets infused in objects from the homes or people they were with. Some objects can have spirits or entities attached to them. This is what I felt when I was in a store with so many antique objects. I felt sick to my stomach and dizzy. When looking at a fan made of feathers for ceremonies, I was told by a stern male voice, *"That isn't yours!"* I said *"OK!"* and put it right down. This spirit didn't scare me because I knew I was safe and didn't feel like he was threatening me, he just didn't want me to take his prized possession. On the other hand, it may have just not been meant for me! Maybe that spirit wanted a specific person to buy that object. I was not privy to that knowledge, and that is ok!

How to use Psychometry:

Begin by choosing an object that you know of and from a loved one or friend. Clear your space, set your intention, raise your vibration, and call in your Divine guides. Then, pick up the object or touch it. Close your eyes and take a breath. Clear your mind. Allow any thoughts to come to your mind or feel the feelings. You may sense that person in your mind's eye standing there right next to you. This is REAL. Don't dismiss anything. You are NOT making it up. You may get a single word or a phrase or you may see a movie playing in your mind of another time or place. You may be catapulted into a scene that is not from your life. This is a natural ability, allow it to flow in. If you don't feel like you receive any information, then come back to the room, ground yourself, and try again another time.

You may also get information the same way by touching someone's hands, shoulder, or body. It's a connection to their soul just like the energetic memories from an object that you are connected to. You may see family members in light standing around them or you may be catapulted into a historical experience from their life. Please note that you do NOT have to touch a person to get psychic information about them but sometimes, it may help.

You may be standing in a place on Earth that holds memories from its existence. I found that I would be standing still on the Earth, and suddenly I could see in my mind's eye, like time-lapse photography, how the Earth looked thousands of years ago, and it would shift and change with the seasons as the Earth shifted. I also saw the past on my property and saw the old farmers, wagons, and animals that occupied the land. It's such an amazing thing to experience! It's like seeing a secret movie from another time that is just for you! To do this, you can simply stand anywhere and ask your spiritual team to help you see what has been there before you. You can put your hands on the Earth, stand there, or simply walk.

Can you think of any experiences you've had where you felt you experienced these? I have experienced many, and I have heard others speak of experiences with these extraordinary abilities!

I spoke of an experience in my first book, You're Not Crazy, You're Simply Divine, an experience where I was out for a walk and a car was about to hit me. My Angels stepped in and suddenly, I felt like I dissolved into a million pieces, then came back to my body. The car had passed, and I was fine. That was bilocation. I didn't do it on my own, but there have been many humans who have mastered these abilities.

A close family member went to Italy for the first time and could speak Italian without ever learning the language in this life. How does that work? Could it be from knowing that language in a past life? Is it a soul memory? These are mysteries that hopefully, someday, we will understand. Better yet, ask your guides! They hold the answers to the Universe! I love to be challenged by clients who ask *Why?!* This is how I have learned so much in the past 8 years, ever since hearing my mother speak to me from the spirit world in 2014. I simply ask my Guides, *"How does this work?"* You'd be surprised at the answers. From Wikipedia, the following lists fun psychic abilities! (Wikipedia n.d.)

Astral projection or mental projection – The ability to voluntarily project an astral body or mental body, being associated with the out-of-body experience, in which one's consciousness is felt to temporarily separate from the physical body.

Automatic writing – The ability to draw or write without conscious intent.

Bilocation — The ability to be present in two different places at the same time, usually attributed to a Saint.

Energy medicine – The ability to heal with one's own empathic, etheric, astral, mental, or spiritual energy.

Ergokinesis – The ability to influence the movement of energy, such as electricity, without direct interaction.

Levitation or transvection – The ability to float or fly by mystical means.

Materialization — The creation of objects and materials or the appearance of matter from unknown sources.

Mediumship or channeling – The ability to communicate with spirits.

Petrification — The power to turn a living being to stone by looking them in the eye.

Prophecy (also prediction, premonition, or prognostication) — the ability to foretell events, without using induction or deduction from known facts.

Psychic surgery – The ability to remove disease or disorder within or over the body tissue via an "energetic" incision that heals immediately afterward.

Psychokinesis or telekinesis – The ability to influence a physical system without physical interaction, typically manifesting as being able to exert force, control objects, and move matter with one's mind.

Pyrokinesis – The ability to control flames, fire, or heat using one's mind.

Iddhi – Psychic abilities gained through Buddhist meditation.

Shapeshifting or transformation — The ability to physically transform the user's body into anything.

Thoughtography – The ability to impress an image by 'burning' it on a surface using one's mind only.

Xenoglossy — The ability of a person to suddenly learn to write and speak a foreign language without any natural means such as studying or research, but that is often rather bestowed by Divine agents.

Witnessing – The gift of being visited by high-profile spiritual beings such as Mary, Jesus, or Fudosama (Acala) from Buddhist traditions.

Inedia - The ability to survive without eating or drinking. Multiple cases have resulted in starvation or dehydration.

Extrasensory perception, or sixth sense – An ability as well as comprising a set of abilities.

Clairvoyance — The ability to see things and events that are happening far away, and locate objects, places, and people by using a sixth sense.

Divination – The ability to gain insight into a situation using occult lists.

Dowsing – The ability to locate water, sometimes using a divination tool called a dowsing rod.

Dream telepathy – The ability to telepathically communicate with another person through dreams.

Dermo-optical perception – The ability to perceive unusual sensory stimuli through one's skin.

Psychometry or psychoscopy – The ability to obtain information about a person or an object by touch.

Precognition (including psychic premonitions) – The ability to perceive or gain knowledge about future events, without using induction or deduction from known facts.

Remote viewing, telesthesia, or remote sensing – The ability to see a distant or unseen target using extrasensory perception.

Retrocognition or post cognition – The ability to supernaturally perceive past events.

Telepathy – The ability to transmit or receive thoughts supernaturally.

Chapter 11

Mediumship

Chapter 11

Mediumship! Working with Human People in Spirit. Did They Cross Over to the Light? Things You NEED to Know!

Human Spirits Who HAVE NOT Crossed Into the Light

When you are a natural medium and psychic, spirit people can be drawn to your light, and they will try to connect with you. It's like you have your flag up on your mailbox saying, *"I'm here! Come to me, and I can help you!"* Since humans are empathic to others, human spirits know that they can make you feel how they do. If they have not crossed over to the light, they will look grey-scale or darker in energy. They will feel heavy with emotions. They may project the way they feel onto you. This is why mediums most often tell you how that person died, and what happened to them as the human spirit makes them feel it or know it. It is imperative that YOU – as a medium – clear the energy that is not your own. You will need to set up firm boundaries with them to not take on their problems. You will set up these boundaries with your Gatekeeper Guide.

Note: We are all natural mediums, psychics, and intuitives. People in spirit can sense this. This may be something you are not aware of. You may have many people in the spiritual dimension around you trying to connect with you and you may be oblivious to this fact. Think of the scene in the movie the Sixth Sense when the young boy is laying in his bed and he says, *"I see dead people."* This happens all the time because people in spirit are all over but we have blocked our ability to see it. The more you open spiritually, the more you will sense, feel, know, hear, taste, and see these things. Some people have raised a bigger flag than others. If you are a caring person that likes to help others, then spirits will be drawn to you for that help. You attract spirits because THEY KNOW YOU CAN HELP THEM. This also happens in the 3D world.

Have you noticed that people come to you and tell you, their problems? This is the same intuitive knowing that they have as the ones in spirit who are in the lower spiritual dimension. They are still intuitive, but they are stuck in a heavy and dense energetic place and need help finding their way. People in life and people in death intuitively know that you are someone who may be able to help them, even if you don't know. This is a sign that you are a light-worker! Please move away from fear. There is nothing to be afraid of. They are just people in another dimension. They are just a person asking for help or trying to get your attention.

Most people's spirits who have not crossed into the light know they are dead, but not all do. If they are confused when they pass, then they may still be confused after they pass. People with traumatic deaths due to quick accidents, tend to be confused and dazed. Ones who were on drugs or severely intoxicated, and people who had Alzheimer's disease, or severe dementia, tend to be confused and stuck in that lower dimension. They may be wandering and you may feel a feeling of confusion and chaos from them. People who have committed suicide may be there as well and are working out their emotions in that space, or wallowing in deep dark emotions. People who have done heinous deeds and crimes may be here. There are many levels of this dimension, some are lighter, and some go down to very dark energy. I DO NOT RECOMMEND that you purposely come to this dimension unless you clear your energy properly. This is not a place full of giggles and fun. The reasons are endless for why some don't cross into the light. Some want revenge, some feel they will go to Hell and since they were taught about writhing in Hell, they do not want to leave this place. Hell doesn't exist. Some dimensions aren't wonderful, but Hell is a construct that was created by humans to keep others from knowing their divinity. I have had many of these spirits tell me they felt they would go to Hell, or don't deserve to go to the light. They do! We are all Divine beings and deserve to go back to our real HOME.

Important note: every human on this planet comes from the light and holds that God-spark within their heart. The human spirits who are in this lower dimension (haven't crossed to the light) have the ability to go to the light, through the pearly gates, and into the healing place with Source, the Angels, and be cleansed from the experiences of the human life on Earth. Mediums act as a bridge between Heaven and Earth, guiding them to Heaven. Some of them are coming to you for that reason! They are done playing in the dark and want to rise into the healing light of Source. You can show them their own inner light (or point it out to them) so they can remember who they are. Even the worst criminals have light in their hearts. They just don't know how to access it.

Spirits that have not crossed over to the light (central sun or Divine light in Heaven) are in a lower vibrational dimension of the upper world, also known as Heaven. I see this as a place located below the pearly gates! It is a series of dimensions below the pearly gates that have many dimensions within itself. This has also been called purgatory.

If spirits haven't crossed over to the light, they may be trying to talk to you, or project their feelings, emotions, and physical pain onto you to let you know what they feel. This can affect you immensely! You can say *"Thank you but this is not my energy. Spirit, please take it away."* If it isn't yours, it will leave immediately. Usually, these spirits are just trying to talk to you. To give you information on how they died or want you to give a loved one information. It's not often that I run into an angry spirit. Don't get me wrong, they DO exist, and they usually make themselves known. As a medium, you have the ability to speak with them and assist them to a better place where they can be healed by their Divine team of light that they are not able to access because they are in such a dark place. You are the guiding light that shows them the way. This is some of the most honoring and rewarding work. To help someone that is feeling like they are in peril, doomed, and stuck, to a bridge to the most Divine place imaginable to get the exact healing and to immediately be healed by the Divine light, and masters of healing are so amazingly rewarding.

You will work with your spirit guide known as your Gatekeeper to give them your preferences on how to work with spirits in this dimension. Do you want to help them? If this scares you, then ask your Gatekeeper Guide to help them to someone else who can help them or to a specialist guide or Angel who helps those in need. By doing so, you will keep yourself, your home, and your private space clear of wandering human spirit people.

I limit how much I work with human spirits that haven't crossed the light, and I always try to assist them to the light or Heavens. THEY HAVE TO CHOOSE TO GO. They have free will just as we do in the human plane. They choose where they want to be.

How to Assist Human Spirits to the Light

All humans are born from the Divine and hold the spark of the Divine within them, centered in the heart chakra. You, the medium, act as the middle person that offers them guidance and, with the help of your spiritual team of light, assistance. If you can see them and they feel dense, heavy with emotion, and void of light, then you can choose to offer your help. You may feel or psychically see these human spirits with your mind's eye or with your naked eye. You may sense someone there with you. If you can't tell if they have crossed over, simply ask your personal Spirit Guides and Angels to let you know. If they sparkle with Divine light and make you feel that energy, they have already crossed over and are healed from their human experiences. If they look heavy, dense, feel depressed, or emit low vibrations, then this usually indicates that they have not crossed over.

What to do to help these spirits cross to the light?

The first thing I do is listen to them, and let them know they are not alone, and that they have helpers waiting to assist them.

I ask for the most Divine helpers to come from the Heavenly realm to come to bring them home. This may be Angels, but that is not necessarily always the case. Remember, human spirits that haven't crossed have had many experiences that caused them to be in this heavy place. They have biases and beliefs from life that make them think that they deserve to be there, they deserve to be in Hell for what they did, or that they aren't deserving of going somewhere better. They sometimes feel they are where they are supposed to be. Sometimes they want to stay angry and bitter. As a medium, I can listen to them by offering a listening ear.

Someone who has had a very bad experience with religion may not be willing to allow the Angels or an Ascended Master such as Jesus to assist them. This is where it is imperative that you ask for whoever is the BEST for that individual to come to show them their way to the light, to Home. Believe me when I say I learned this the hard way!

Many times, when they are not willing to work with Angels, I see dear family members coming into the room with them. It is usually a most joyous occasion. You cannot mess up doing this since your spiritual team is working with theirs to bring in those who are the best candidates to help them. They know much more than we do. One specific client I worked with had an older lady that was connected with her family member. I had tried before to get her to go to the light with no avail. I had previously asked the Angels to come in, but she wasn't comfortable with them. The next time was around a year later, and I was guided to ask this way instead of just asking the Angels. This time a very young puppy dog made up of golden and white light came in, and she reverted to a childlike self. A door opened with a light behind it and she walked in! It was so amazing!

I also had another experience with a man that was on a friend's property. Everyone had tried to get him to go to the light with no avail. I simply went into a light meditative state and went to him. He seemed to be stuck in a loop of what he did in his life and didn't want to leave that place. I asked for his most Divine helpers to come in. This man lived 200 years ago and worked this land. All his relatives were crossed. They stepped in as a family. His granddaughter stepped in, arms wide open, and he dropped what he was doing. He rushed to the arms of his grandchild and was so happy to be with her. He said he was stuck and didn't realize how much he had missed her. He stood up and hugged his whole family, there were about 10 of them. The light behind them was a blinding white light, and they turned around as a family and walked into that light. He had crossed. They took him Home.

You can do this work by creating a door of light that connects to the light of Source. Imagine creating a door with your mind, just draw it! It is a portal of energy that is a bridge to the Divine light they came from. When they go in, they go across the pearly gates (which also have a Gate Master) and to a healing place with Angels, master healers, spiritual counselors, and much more. They go through many phases of healing and review the life they have just experienced many times. They go through a detoxification of the human physical world. When they have completed these stages, they are full of Divine light and joy and sparkle when you see them. They then become human spirits who HAVE crossed into the light.

I have had so many amazing experiences doing this work. I am honored each and every time I assist people to find their true home and loving place filled with Divine helpers and spirit family.

Human Spirits Who HAVE Crossed into the Light:

Human spirits that HAVE crossed into the light are a whole different story than those who have not. These spirits are guided by the Divine, and they offer knowledge, wisdom, and help to us as humans.

They may be ancestors who are there to help you on your path or just helpers in general. After crossing over to the light, they have gone through a thorough spiritual cleansing and healing process that far exceeds the abilities of healing on our 3D side of the veil. They go through strict teaching and enlightenment practices with their Divine helpers to be able to assist us. Our spirit guides are usually human helpers who take on that role for you in the same way.

For spirits that have not crossed over yet, you need to have firm boundaries since they have not been cleansed and healed.

In my experience, spirits that have crossed over have free rein. They don't bother you or push boundaries. I give them free rein to assist me and help me on my journey. They are balanced and offer light. They assist us in the 3D world in so many ways like giving us encouragement and guidance.

Do what feels right for you! If they are sparkly and feel wonderful, then they are just fine! Go with your gut feeling!

Chapter 12

Meet Your Higher-Self and Spirit Guides

Chapter 12

Let's Meet Your Higher-Self and Spirit Guides!

Your Spiritual Team Awaits!

This is one of my favorite things to assist my clients to do! Let's meet your spiritual guides! They are our specialized spiritual teams of light, assigned to you, BY you to help you to stay on the path and live a life full of joy, excitement, peace, adventure, and fun! Envision that they are standing next to you and they are your best friends because they are! They are here to always help and guide you. Many of them have been with you since birth and they are your soul family helping from the other side. They have many tools to help you on your life's journey. They are there for you at all times and help you by showing you guidance and love when you most need it. This is the beginning of so many beautiful connections to your soul family. They are usually there with you for life. Some may come and go as you excel in your spiritual growth, and that is normal! You may have guides that were there to help you through a particularly tough time in life. When you don't need them anymore, they may leave. You will upgrade and shift just like being in school. As you grow, you may need a new teacher, and when you need them, they show up! Think of it like grade school, middle school, high school, and college. Where do you think you are on your spiritual journey? You may have Master Teacher Guides already. When I met my spiritual guidance team, the books I read told me that the Spiritual Masters wouldn't usually be a regular spirit guide for me. That was in the old energy. The energy on Earth now is stronger and at a higher vibration. We need help from more masterful guides now. You may meet Jesus as a guide, or an Ascended Master. That is normal now. Don't feel like you are beneath them. They are merely teachers helping you in a most amazing time of the likes of which we have never seen on Earth before. Think of yourself as part of an elite team of humans who are receiving Divine training from them to help the world ascend into a better place for all.

My spiritual guides tell me to call them my team. I grew up playing softball and was a pitcher from 8 years old until 40. My spiritual guides show me that they are around me and working with me just like my softball team surrounded me on the pitching mound. This is a metaphor for how they work. Imagine what that looks like! I have a catcher, and I'm the pitcher. I have a first, second, and third baseman, a shortstop, and three outfielders. We all must work as a team to do our jobs. As a pitcher, I am the one who begins and pitches each ball. I have control, and you have control. I decide when I'm ready to begin, and you do as well. If one person falls apart, the others are there to pick you up, to have your back! You can't control what happens during the game, but you have control of many things, and they are assisting you. You have a say in what you want! Working with your guides will let them know what your preferences are and what is comfortable for you, and what is not. This is especially true when you can see or sense a human spirit (mediumship abilities). If you are not comfortable with this, you may let your Gatekeeper Guide know that you are not comfortable with that, and they will assist you.

You will normally go into a meditative state or journey to meet them, but not always. I had experiences where I instantly downloaded information from my guides while in an awake state. This was a light meditative state, also known as a walking meditative state. Allow this information to come in whenever it's supposed to. Many times, spiritual "downloads" of information come in when you least expect it. My main spiritual guide, Franklin, answered my question one day when I wondered what my main guide's name was. I was cleaning my house and just randomly thought in my mind, *"I wonder what my main guide's name is?"* I got an immediate answer – Franklin! I thought that was too good to be true, it couldn't come that easily! And then I heard him talking to me like we were just having a friendly conversation. I jokingly asked if I could call him Frank, and he got very serious and said NO. He was serious but in a joking way. He was serious for a few seconds, then laughed. He then showed me that he was ME from a past lifetime. What a beautiful experience!

When people say they wished they had multiple versions of themselves to do all the things they need to do, I chuckle because we do have many versions of ourselves and many times, they are our guides who hold wisdom, knowledge, and life experiences that help guide us on our journey. They are knowledgeable assets to us as humans! It's a system made for us to connect all the parts of ourselves through all time and space, and this makes it possible to spiritually connect and heal other parts of ourselves. It's like a buddy system within layers of yourself you never knew existed! Imagine having all that help! These helpers have been there helping and assisting without you knowing. That is the helpful voice of reason in your head when you lose your cool. That is the voice that helps you come to reason when you feel lost. That is the arrow pointing you in the right direction when you are stuck trying to decide which way to go in life. They help guide us back on track. Now, you get to meet them! Thank them for all the assistance they have given you. Tell them you're sorry when you didn't listen.

You will need to raise your vibration to meet them. Your spiritual guides come from a higher dimension than our Earthly plane so you must raise your vibration to meet them. Please refer to Chapters 3 and 4 on how to clear your space, create sacred space, and raise your vibration. This work may seem like you are making it up. When you have these feelings, brush them away. Take a breath and let those feelings go. This work FEELS like you are making it up. We aren't always taught to trust and listen to ourselves in our culture. To do this work, you must open to a world you haven't allowed yourself to trust. If you try and don't obtain much information, then it isn't the right time. If you get frustrated, irritated, or sad, then it acts as a block. You must be in a higher vibrational state of mind to do this amazing work. Allow yourself to rise to a higher dimension. You should feel floaty and light, full of buzzing energy that feels delicious and free. As I write this book, I feel that way now! It is a pure connection to the Divine. The energy of Source runs through you. It fills you up with pure loving energy from the Heavens, and from the Earth. You BELONG here! The feeling of euphoria I speak of is your proof. Allow it in, and revel in that bliss. It's a happy state of being, and you deserve it!

Remember, they are your soul family! You asked them to assist you. You can trust them. Ask their names, write down what they look like, feel like, and how they make you feel. Get to know them. They are always around you waiting to assist you. Make sure you journal all the information you receive. You will not always remember the details.

Please note that these are not the only guides you may have. Remember, this is your soul family! You may have guides that have different roles than what is listed here. We are all unique and have different needs for spiritual guides, allies, and helpers. For me, I have many protector guides including spirit animals that help keep me safe while clearing negative energies from people and places. Because of this, I have a huge entourage of spirit animals, Angels, spiritual protector guides, Archangels, and much more.

Important Notes:

*Spirit guides may also be animals, otherworldly beings such as an elf, fae (faery realm being), goddess, or something you've never seen before. Keep a VERY open mind. Spirit work may seem wild and beyond your imagination, and for a very good reason! It is fun and exciting! See where it takes you!

*When asking your spiritual guides questions, be very specific with the way you ask your question. When you ask a vague question, you get a vague answer and it may not be what you meant to ask.

*When asking spiritual guides for guidance, they will most often answer for what gives you more soul growth, which may not feel like they are helping you at all. Know that the soul growth they guide you towards will help you fulfill your purpose and destiny on Earth. You may question that guidance at times for this reason. My guides call this a detour on your path that helps you learn what you need to, then they redirect you on that path. When being redirected, you may find that what you thought you wanted wasn't in your best interest. It is then that you find your new path opens and you move onto that new path happily and heartily.

Set your intention that only the most loving being of light that is of the highest vibration is welcome as a spiritual guide/ally/helper, and that is what you shall receive.

Spiritual Guides
Roles for Spirit Guides: Spirit Helpers and Guides

Spirit Helpers and Guides all have specialties, talents, and knowledge from their life experiences that make them perfect for the role of your guide. Each one of them has had their own experiences through many lifetimes that have provided them with the understanding of what you may be going through. They have been there and done that, and therefore, are a wonderful teacher for you and what you are going through. They have the experience and they can relate to you in what you are going through. For example, a joy guide may be someone who has learned to let go of most of their traumas and live in the joy of the moment and is very in touch with the happy and uninhibited parts of themselves like a free-spirited child. They may even show themselves to you as a child. They will teach you to explore and play as you did as a child. The Gatekeeper Guide is a very old soul that understands how to keep you safe and has a mastery level of knowledge to be esteemed in that position. Your Protector Guide may have been a warrior or guard who knows how to protect you from the many lifetimes of training in that field. If you are interested in different subjects such as art, music, dance, or even the art of war, then you may have a guide for that. If you haven't already, you can ask for one. This is the beauty of this work!

Spirit Guides are different than Angels. There are many different types of Angels, and I recommend learning about them. We all have guardian angels, healing angels, and protector angels, and they are NOT human. Human spirits and guides are not the same as Angels, but they may act like Angels. Angels may guide you as well but they are different beings.

Main Guide: This would be your main Spirit Guide. This Guide has almost always been a human and has lived many incarnations so they can be a guide for others. We choose our spirit guides before we come into the physical incarnation. Often, they are other versions of ourselves (from past or future lifetimes), or a dear friend that helps us from the other side to make decisions. The Main Guide is most often a spokesperson for all the guides and is a leader of your spiritual guide team. They speak for all when they answer you. They gather all the wisdom from all of your guides to compile the best guidance for you on your spiritual path.

Gatekeeper Guide: Also known as your mediumship guide. They are the guides on the other side who oversee organizing the human spirits that would like to speak to you. They need a lot of interaction and instruction on what you want, when, where, and how. They keep the negative entities out and keep order for human spirits. Let them know you don't want spirits bugging you all night, keeping you up. Set times during the day with them to work with spirits. They dual as a protector by not allowing anything but those who walk in the light to work with you. They are the number 1 guide to meet so you can stay safe, especially if you are working with people in spirit. I see this guide as one who is like a bouncer at a club, who allows in certain people and doesn't let others in. YOU DECIDE WHO IS ALLOWED IN YOUR SPACE. When meeting your Gatekeeper Guide, they will ask what your preferences are. As I explained in Chapter 11, human spirits can hold different vibrations.

The next one is also a big must to start working with as they are your protector. Your Gatekeeper could be the same guide as your Protector Guide. They work together to help keep you safe.

Protector Guide: Your Protector Guide may be large and stocky, someone who is trained to protect in life, such as a ninja, guard, or fighter. They will stay around your energy field. For example, mine looks like a very large Polynesian warrior who guards me from the front. I also have two ninjas that guard me from the back and sides. The ninjas are small but mighty. They can also be spirit animals who oversee keeping you safe. I personally have more than usual because of the dark energy I transmute. They will present themselves to you and many times bow to you in honor of being your protector. Think of them as your bodyguards who are keeping harsh entities and energies away from you. They are master fighters in the spiritual realms and dimensions and work with your spirit animals to guard and protect you at all times, especially when you don't realize you need it. You may have more than one protector guide, and they may show themselves to you AS a spirit animal or change their appearance back and forth from animal to guardian. For example, they may first appear as a wolf, and then, shift into a fierce male warrior. Your Protector Guide may also show themselves as female as women hold just as much power as men.

Doctor Teacher/Shamanic/Witch Guide/Medical Intuitive Guide: You can have more than one, and sometimes mine show me many versions of themselves as many experiential lifetimes provide them the knowledge to assist you. This is your resource for most of the information about your clients. This guide, or these guides if more than one, helps you to obtain information about your client's physical, emotional, or energetic problems. They will assist you in helping the client to heal in many ways. Doctor Guides may show you that they lived lifetimes as medical doctors. I have a male spirit guide that shows himself to me as an older male from the 1800s and shows me his black leather medical bag that he carried everywhere. It is full of old-fashioned glass bottles and potions, along with old-fashioned medical tools. A Shamanic Guide may be a shaman from a native tribe anywhere in the world that shows you scenes of ancient rituals and healings that he or she performed to help heal someone from a physical or emotional ailment. A Witch Guide may show you that they were known as a witch but was very gifted herbal healer from a time hundreds of years in the past. He or she may show you how they connected to the Earth, see between dimensions, and see faery or other interdimensional beings. He or she may have been a Master Healer by using ancient techniques of hands-on healing much like reiki. A Medical Intuitive Guide may show you any of these types of experiences as a shaman, psychic seer, oracle, or Ascended Master such as Jesus, Mary Magdalene, Buddha, or Mother Mary, who are all Master Teachers and are here to guide you with advanced healing techniques. I personally received a Doctor Guide who showed me herself as a female doctor from the 1960s, and she was very helpful in getting me started on my journey. As I gained knowledge and experience, I received an Ascended Master Guide that came to help me as I encountered more challenging healings and clearings. If you are better with one subject than another, then you may have a team of guides. For me, I have all of them as guides since I specialize in mediumship, medical intuition, and shamanism.

Chemist/Alchemist Guides: These guides are just what it sounds like! They help you tap into your inner magic and mystical gifts! Don't be surprised if this guide is a very well-known Ascended Master or wizard/priestess. These guides are so amazing to work with and help you on so many levels, and along with that, they are a blast and teach you all kinds of esoteric lessons that may be lost in the shuffle of time and space. They help you bring back your spiritual gifts, open them up, and learn how to work with them. They will show you that you have Divine skills that you can learn to tap back into. They can help you bend time and energy, and they will show you how to work and play with energy. They are so much fun to work with! They help you become a Master Healer, teacher, and alchemist.

Joy Guides: Your Joy Guides oversee helping you to find your spark and keep it. They help you keep your vibration high, and how to look on the brighter side of things in your life. Joy guides are fun and loving, and they have a very high vibration. They help you take time for yourself and not work yourself too hard. Many times, they show themselves as a child since they represent and help you tap into your inner childlike self. They may be adventurous, mischievous, loving, carefree, and over the top. They are there to help you lighten up and get you out of the doldrums. They are there to show you new ways of thriving in life and living the life of your dreams. They will help you shed beliefs that you need to be unhappy to live and that you do not need to be suffering while on Earth. They show you ways of changing your belief system to realize that you are here to live in harmony and happiness. They usually have a glow about them because they represent pure light and joy. They help you remember things that make you glow and help you on your path to reconnect to that part of yourself again. They teach you to find a way to play again!

Ascended Master Guides: Ascended Master Guides are so important. They are Ascended Masters who have graduated from living physical lives unless they choose to come back to Earth and help with the ascension process. They are a wealth of knowledge and help us work towards enlightenment and mastery.

They can be instrumental in helping us to tap into better choices in life and take the higher road. They help us when we are stuck in our old paradigms and come out to us at a higher frequency when we make better choices.

You may have Ascended Master Guides you haven't heard of. They may be from ancient, advanced communities on Earth, from different times such as Ancient MU, Lemuria, Atlantis, and

Egypt where they acted as Master Healers, seers, or deities (gods or goddesses). They have a wealth of knowledge and have lived so many lifetimes that they have ascended to a higher level of consciousness and no longer need to incarnate on Earth. They can choose if they want to incarnate into a human body. Their main purpose is to guide the ones who must still incarnate and have human experiences. They teach us to be spiritual masters. Think of Earth as a school. The Ascended Master Guides have been to this school and graduated. They are now the professors showing us better ways.

There are so many Ascended Masters, I could never name them all. Some are known as Gods or Goddesses. Some of my personal Ascended Master Guides are Mother Mary, Jesus, Mary Magdalene, Mahavatar Babaji, Buddha, Isis, Green Tara, Quan Yin, Anna, grandmother of Jesus, and many more. I recommend learning about these Divine helpers. Learn who they are, and what they went through. They hold so many answers for us!

Higher Self: Your Higher Self is our main "us" that is the highest form of ourselves, has no lower vibrations, and is just pure love energy. The chakra above our heads is where our Higher Self resides. Connect with your Higher Self to get answers for anything. We only bring a very small percentage of our true energy and most of it resides within our Higher Self. Throughout your life, as you do your spiritual work, you will download higher percentages of your Higher Self and incorporate it into your energy field, thus raising your vibration and elevating your energetic DNA. When this happens, you may feel euphoric and full of Divine heavenly energy and light. You can envision this as a DNA strand that has missing pieces and the Higher Self drops in the ancient codes of light that contain energetic keys that activate those missing pieces. Doing this sacred work is slowly activating your energetic DNA. As you activate this more and more, you are able to access your spiritual abilities. You become more psychic. Simply put, you just know things. Your Higher Self and your Ascended Master Guides help you to accelerate the spiritual path. They are also loving and Divine helpers from the Heavenly realms that are there to assist you in who you came here to be!

Specialist Guides: You may call on guides for a variety of situations. One I like to work with is my Business Guide. Other options may vary. You can ask for a Specialist Guide for any situation you can think of! I asked for a Specialist Guide to help me figure out a tough billing job I was having a hard time with. After she came in, I magically knew things and understood how to do my job with ease. This guide looked to me like a typical 1960s or 1970s secretary that had a big bouffant hairstyle, she chewed gum and popped bubbles loudly, had clothing of that era, and had long fingernails that clicked loudly on her typewriter. She was fun, goofy, and to the point. After she came in to assist me, I noticed that answers to things that didn't make sense to me came with ease. This fun-loving guide is still with me and helps me with my business. She is a comic relief when I am frustrated.

If you are in a pickle and having a hard time with something, ask for a Specialist Guide to come to help! They can help with jobs, personal life, driving, parking, planning a vacation, and planning a wedding or party. The sky is the limit!

Guided Meditation

Chapter 13

Guided Meditation to Meet Your Spirit Team!

Let's begin on your journey to meet your Spirit Guides, Angels, and ancestors that are in the light! This is the method you can use to rise into this high vibrational plane of existence over and over to meet with your spiritual team. Don't try to meet them all at once! It may take many meditations to meet them all. Please do this in moderation when you are ready to meet them. They will appear.

1. Clear your space, set your intentions, get cozy, and comfortable, and make sure you won't have any distractions from animals, children, friends, or your spouse! This work is very important! Please remember to journal each time you do this work.

2. Please make sure to be physically comfortable as you may want to just melt into your bed within this blissful state, and if you feel like you are floating on a cloud energetically, you need to feel like you're on a bed of feathers in the physical world. You don't want a painful body to keep you from achieving the higher states of consciousness that you need to do this work. Use lots of pillows, cushions, and a crystal-infused heated mat to lay on if you have one.

3. Call your spiritual entourage to come to assist you on this journey! Feel the energy shift when you call them. The air feels cleaner and lighter and may sizzle with an energy that buzzes all around you.

4. Call your Divine Angels, your Higher Self, your spirit animals, and helpers within the realms of light that are here for you.

5. Perform 5 repetitions of deep, slow breath in, hold for 5 seconds, and slowly release the air from your lungs. Envision that the breath releases tension and uncoils it until it flows from you through your breath, and dissolves into sparkling dust as it leaves your mouth.

6. Slowly relax and let your breathing shift into a nice, slow rhythm. Deep breaths in, and relaxing breaths out. Feel yourself begin to relax more and more as you feel yourself dip lower and lower into a delicious sense of heavy relaxation. Allow any tension that you feel in your body to just melt and evaporate from your body.

7. Begin to focus on your breathing, and the coolness of the air that flows into your nostrils. Follow the flow of breath coming into your lungs, and out through your mouth. Follow the stream of the breath as it comes in through your crown and your tiny spiritual antennae that are a part of your light body. Feel these feelers of light sparkle with anticipation of the Divine energy from the sun, the stars, and the Divine that receive the luminescent energy of joy from the Heavens and Mother Earth. As you breathe, envision this fluid energy flowing into and through your light body, spreading throughout. Inhale it, welcome it, and let it sizzle through your body until you feel like you are lit up. See the energy from above and below swirl together in your heart space. Now, focus on your heart space with the glow of light that radiates from it. Notice now what color that glowing heart space is. Take a breath in and expand that light from your heart in all directions and around you, throughout your entire auric field in a circle or oval 5 to 10 feet around you.

8. You are now glowing from the inside out and it comes from your heart! You are connected to the Divine Father from above, the Divine Mother from below, and your spiritual team of light that is ever so willing to meet you. Connect with the spiritual antennae that are coming from your light body and plug it in in all directions to the Divine.

9. You should feel light and free, soaring with Divine light and love running through your whole body. You may feel tingles and energetic pulses running through your body. Allow this Divine connection with your soul family. They are here as you rise in consciousness to meet with you in a Divine place of light, illumination, peace, and harmony.

10. Look around you. You have just shifted into another dimension which is within the light of your heart to meet with your spiritual family. You may see blinding light. If you are blinded by this light, wait a few seconds to acclimate to that light. It's much like going outside from a dark room on a very sunny day and being blinded by the light for a few minutes. You simply need to let your senses adjust to this glorified Divine space that was custom-made for you and by your Higher Self.

11. As your vision adjusts to the light, it seems to tone down so you may be able to view your surroundings. This is the space from within your heart, which is a door to your Divine spiritual team. Think of your sacred heart space as a meeting space, a safe place where they are allowed to visit you. You may call it your heart garden, your heart sanctuary, or your heart vacation destination! This is a place that your Higher Self created, just for you, and you can change it in any way you like. Take time now to envision and create your most decadent place of joy, harmony, peace, and contentment. You are SAFE here. You are supported. You are loved.

12. Allow yourself to create waterfalls, elaborate and colorful gardens, crystal mansions, and temples of gold. Create it with your mind as you walk through this place of harmony. There may be animals frolicking around and playing, some may look solid, and some may look crystalline. You create the scenery, the sounds, the weather, and the smells in your sacred heart space.

Birds may sing in the background, or you may hear Angels singing in glorious harmony. You may be in a place that looks like Atlantis, with golden buildings and structures built in circular patterns on the water. There may be mermaids, whales, and dolphins swimming all around you.

13. Use every sense you have to create this masterpiece of a place that resides in your heart space. Feel the softness of the grass under your feet, smell the fragrance of the flowers you see, dig your feet into the soft grass, and FEEL the coolness of it. Allow your imagination to run wild, it is your place of peace and it is here for you any time you need to go within.

14. Take your time building this space and getting comfortable here. As you journey through this place, you will notice that there is no gravity. You can fly, you can lift and hover over the ground by just thinking it into existence. Take a breath in, and on the out-breath, you can jump to the top of a building, or lift off into the sky to fly. Use your breath and thoughts to soar in the air. Flying with the wind is easy.

15. When you are done exploring and creating this beautiful place, go to the space that you created to meet with your spiritual team. This can be in a temple, on a cloud, or simply in a garden.

16. Invite your Divine spiritual team to come to meet you. They may come as a team and step up one at a time to meet you, or

they may come in one at a time so that you can have the experience of meeting them individually.

<u>Please note</u>: Angels can come to you in this place of light as well. You will need to be able to raise your vibration to meet them.

17. Ask for your guides to meet with you. Here is a list of possible spirit guides for you:

> Your Higher Self – which is the orchestrator of your life and resides in the chakra above your crown chakra.
> Main Spirit Guide – your overseer.
> Gatekeeper Guide – helps you to keep out energies, and entities, and keeps control of spirits that want to talk to you. Spend a lot of time with this Guide to set your boundaries on what you want to experience.
> Protector Guide – many times this can be an animal and can be someone who has the training to be a guardian for you.
> Doctor Guide
> Teacher Guide
> Shamanic Guide
> Witch Guide
> Medical Intuitive Guide
> God or Goddess Guide – this could be from mythology or someone you have heard of.
> Chemist/Alchemist Guide
> Joy Guide
> Ascended Master Guide
> Specialist Guides – You may ask for specific Specialist Guides as well.
> Angels
> Archangels

18. As you meet these Divine helpers, get as much information about them as possible. What do they look like? What are they wearing? What is their name? What qualifies them to be a guide, and what type of guide are they? Anything you can think of, ask them! That is what they are here for. They will be very open and honest with you. They are here to serve you while you take this soul journey to Earth. They are your team behind the curtain, so to speak. They are helping you in so many ways. Get to know them in this space.

If you focus too hard to get details, then let go of that, take a deep breath, and focus lightly on something else, such as their feet, or hands. You don't need to know everything about them, and you may not see them clearly in your mind's eye.

You may just feel them there. You may not SEE anything. Allow yourself to be shown in different ways that they are there. You may smell flowers or grass. You may have a sense of a loving hug from someone you can't see. If you ask your guides to come in, then they are there! If all you get is blobs of color in your mind's eye, then that is how you sense them.

Many times, I see spirit guides as white or different-colored beings made of light. I ask them to tone down the brightness so I can see them. Then I can make out what looks like a face. Have patience with yourself! If you get stuck, let the frustration go, and ask them to show you something else. When you least expect it, you will see, or receive what you wanted to!

19. Please don't forget to thank them for doing all the work they do to help you.

20. When you are finished, say goodbye, and call your energy back to your physical body. You can simply call it back and bring

yourself down in a tube of light. Take a deep breath in and as you exhale, feel yourself coming back down from that higher vibration, bringing your energy back into your physical body. Repeat the deep breath in and exhale until you have brought all your energy back into your physical body.

21. Ground your energy into the ground with roots that dig very deep and anchor them into the Earth with your mind's eye, then back up through your body to the Heavens. Next, bring the energy back to your heart, and out through your arms and legs, around the Earth circling East to West, then South to North. Bring that energy back to your heart space that is filled with light, joy, and peace. Take a deep breath, feel your energy come back to your body, and when you are ready, stretch your body and open your eyes.

Please make sure you write everything you can remember in your journal. Think of every detail you can remember, even if it seems like it didn't make any sense to you, or if you didn't think it was important.

Slowly sit up, stretch, and move your body. Make sure to drink water as this helps you to ground yourself.

SPIRITUAL ETIQUETTE

Chapter 14

Spiritual Etiquette, How to be Aware When Channeling Spirit

It is very important to practice common sense when working with Spirit. I have had personal experiences that I wish I could go back in time and change. I gave messages from a husband's spirit to his wife, but I never asked if she wanted to receive a message from him. It's like offering unsolicited advice, and sometimes, it isn't well received. Luckily, that experience was fine, but it had the potential to be a disaster.

Have you had experiences where you gave someone advice when they never asked for your opinion? Was it well received? Did it rub them the wrong way? Maybe that person felt like you were telling them how to live their life or you were butting your nose in where it didn't belong.

The world of spirit isn't much different. Everyone has free will and ideas that have been shaped by life experiences, religion, cultures, and belief systems. As you spiritually expand and can receive messages from Spirit, you will want to learn to use discernment in what messages are appropriate and when they are appropriate to relay to someone who is living.

Being a medium is a God-given gift. In my experience, it has helped me to heal from the deaths of my family members. It gave me closure and let me know that they were in very wonderful ways where they were. They helped me to hone this gift of being a medium. Spirit shows me, when I do readings for others, how they are always talking to family members. They show themselves to me, chatting in their ears, or sending a message in a bubble of light to them.

Our ancestors and family members are part of our spiritual team. They know us so well and can give us a kernel of hope when we need it. On the other hand, it could scare someone who isn't ready to be on the receiving end of that message. It could turn them farther away from Spirit if they have strong beliefs against mediums and psychic abilities. In my opinion, a good medium will plant seeds of hope and light. If they are interested and when they are ready, then let them be their own judge to decide what they are ready for. I now try my very best to offer my channeled spiritual advice only when asked for, or it has been agreed upon by the recipient.

~~~

Exercise

Rules from Spirit to Help You Discern Whether a Message is Appropriate:

1. Is the person to whom you have a message for is willing or accepting of the message?

This was my first mistake when I was given a very important message from a friend that wanted his wife to know he was sorry. I pondered whether she would think I was crazy and pondered if I really was crazy! When he asked me to tell her this information, he was not crossed over and had terrible remorse for leaving her in a bad situation.

This happened when I didn't have any training with mediumship. I felt she would want to know, so I waited until I saw her in person, when I felt it was the right time, and told her the message.

If I could do it all over, I would have asked her a very simple question… "I have a message for you from your deceased husband, are you open to hearing that message?"

2. Is this message appropriate in the setting you are in?

I have had this many times and as a medical intuitive, I learned right away that I may get very personal information for people that is not appropriate for anyone else listening. Ask yourself and your guides if the message is appropriate with others around, even a close family member. Sometimes, that close family member shouldn't hear something very sensitive to the recipient. Spirit knows so much and may reveal something sensitive that family members or friends are not aware of. This can cause problems for them. This is something that taught me a big lesson at the beginning of my channeling journey.

If you have a message such as this, always ask them if they are open to a message from Spirit, and if it is personal, let them know that you have a message for them and it's sensitive. Tell them privately.

3. Do you want to do readings with family members in the room? If so give them a disclaimer.

As I have said, this can be a bad situation for your client if something comes up that they don't want revealed. Let them know ahead of time that this may be the case. Some mediums don't let family members come in with them for a reading. This is why. Secrets may be revealed. I let people make their own decisions. If you let them know this ahead of time, then you leave them to make that decision.

4. Don't approach people in stores or the public. Set some boundaries!

Once you begin to open to Spirit, you have a big giant flag for Spirit that says that you are open for business. For many people, this is the case even when they don't know they are a medium, and they feel overwhelmed with feelings and emotions from Spirit. Spirit will hang out around people who have this ability, whether they know how to use it or not.

You will begin to get all kinds of information while awake and even during sleep. This is where you need to create boundaries with your Gatekeeper Guide to help you keep this under control.

I noticed this for myself when I would be sleeping and receiving information on my clients for the next day. I nipped that in the bud right away by asking my guides to stop giving me information night and day. I set specific times for that to happen. I chose not to be "open for business" when I am in my free time. It can be exhausting. You can't be a medium for everyone, all the time!

5. Use discernment with messages from Spirit.

Can you think of a situation in your life that made you feel uncomfortable when someone told you something you weren't ready to hear? When you are channeling spirit, they may have a lot to say, and it may be of great importance to relay that message to the living recipient. Is this message appropriate? Is that Spirit in the light, or are they in the lower dimensions and full of anger? This could be someone that didn't cross over to the light, and they have a bone to pick with that person. You could say that these people are haunted by a spirit. There are so many scenarios that could play out with people living and dead. If you feel negative energy from a messenger, then you are not dealing with someone who is in the light.

6. Sometimes you will get messages warning of danger.

I have had a handful of times where I was told that my client was in danger with a spouse or boyfriend/girlfriend. In these cases, my parents came in and gave me stern instructions to let them know. It can be very hard to relay these types of messages, but I felt it was my job to tell them what I was being told. My parents coming in for a reading is rare, but they know I will listen, after all, they are my parents! They impressed upon me the severity of the message so these clients could be prepared and be safe. This doesn't mean that all the clients will believe that the one that they love could be a danger to them. Over time, I know that these clients were shown that they were in fact in danger, whether it was emotional danger or physical danger. When you get these messages from beings in the light, listen, and try to find a way to relay that message in a way that doesn't cause the recipient too much fear. When this happened to me, my Guides (parents in this case) were very serious and stern when they told me, which is unlike them. I would rather have that person hear me and have that knowledge than ignore it and have them injured.

I have also felt extreme danger when walking into work in a back alley one early morning. It was dark, I was alone, and I had a deep nagging feeling that I was in danger of walking into work by myself. Trust these feelings. They are naturally intuitive feelings that your spiritual team is giving you to let you know something is not right and to be cautious and aware. I have also had these experiences more and more with a little voice telling me not to drive a certain path to my destination. I heard a voice in my head say, *"DON'T GO THAT WAY!"* Learn to listen to these messages. They are important!

7. Divine spiritual guidance will NEVER be negative. They are LOVING.

Your loving spiritual team of light will never tell you to harm yourself or anyone else. They may show you tough love at times to help you see reality, but they will NEVER give you negative messages unless you or your client are in serious danger. This message is very, very important. If you have guidance that is negative and makes you feel depressed, angry, bitter, or suicidal, then you are not talking to a loving and high-vibrational spirit guide. You are either receiving a message from a person in spirit that is angry, or you are getting messages from an entity that is NOT of the light.

If this is the case, quickly stand your ground, shine your light from within your heart out like the sun, and ask Archangel Michael, any Angel, or Ascended Master to remove this being from your energy field. Remember, you have power, and you are the master of your energy field. Nothing and no one is allowed in your space that you do not allow.

8. Use good judgment when doing this sacred work. Are you in a good place to be giving messages? Is the timing right?

If you are not feeling like yourself or are in a funk and you get spiritual guidance, wait until you are in a better mood before you relay the message.

If anything feels 'off' or not quite right, then shake off the messages and let your spiritual team know to come back another time. This happened to me when a client had a negative spiritual attachment and we both needed our energy cleared prior to giving her any spiritual guidance. This is also a quick reminder to always clear your own energy before doing any spiritual work.

If you sense negative energy attached to a person, don't attempt to work with them if you don't have the spiritual tools yet to clear that from them. This could be negative energies or entities that exist in the space they live or work.

Chapter 15

Angels

Chapter 15

Angels, Who Are They and How Can You Connect with Them? Climbing the Ascension Ladder to Work with Them! Tuning Your Psychic Hearing Through Your Ear Chakras.

Angels definition by Merriam Webster is:

an·gel; ˈān-jəl, plural angels

1. religion: a spiritual being serving as a Divine messenger and intermediary and often as a special protector of an individual or nation. (Merriam-Webster n.d.)

According to Hazel Raven, author of the book *Angel Bible*:

Angels are winged messengers. The word 'Angel' is derived from the ancient Greek angelos, meaning "messenger." Angels act as a bridge between Heaven and Earth, serving as a channel between God and the physical material world. They are beings of pure consciousness, unlimited by the constrictions of time and space. (Raven 2006)

In my experience, Angels may show themselves as winged beings, but I see them mostly as beings of light, and sometimes just as ribbons of light and color. They show themselves to me in many ways. Sometimes I see them as a flame of energy because they are such a high dimensional being of light that they reflect that in my mind's eye.

There are many different types of Angels. We all have Guardian Angels, who work with us and help guide us on our Earthly journey. Hundreds of thousands of Angels form into groups to join forces for humanity.

According to Wikipedia, the most influential Christian angelic hierarchy was that put forward by Pseudo-Dionysius the Areopagite in the 5th or 6th century in his book *De Coelesti Hierarchia (On the Celestial Hierarchy)*. Dionysius described nine levels of spiritual beings which he grouped into three orders: (Wikipedia n.d.)

Vibrational Order of Angels from Highest to lowest:

Highest Orders

    Seraphim
    Cherubim
    Thrones

Middle Orders

    Dominions
    Virtues
    Powers

Lowest Orders

    Principalities
    Archangels
    Angels

The Angels I have worked with the most are Guardian Angels, Angels (who hold a very wide variety of jobs), Archangels, and Seraphim Angels. When doing spiritual healing, I work and channel these high vibrational beings. The energy that they send through (channeling) is very intense and it is amazing to feel the power and love they emanate. I love to work with my clients' healing Angels. They are powerful energy healers and help to cleanse your light body and spiritually activate your spiritual DNA.

I can never say this enough – YOU MUST GIVE ANGELS PERMISSION TO WORK WITH YOU, OR THEY CANNOT HELP YOU (except in times of peril or emergency).

I can feel and psychically see Angels daily while doing this Divine work. I can't say that I know what order they all are, but I know they are loving and Divine, and it is such a blessing to be able to say I can sense them. They are everywhere! You simply need to be open and accepting of them. They are helping you behind the spiritual veils. They are the helpers that reside just out of sight for us. They carry out and accomplish magical and Divine work! They perform miracles and help us out of situations that we could not imagine!

Guardian Angels: We all have Guardian Angels that have been with us since birth. They are always with you and that is their purpose. I usually see two with each person. My guides tell me that is because we need extra help in these times. I am usually working with light workers and they need extra help to work on themselves and to spiritually wake up. They help you with all the little things like finding a parking place, shopping, cooking, and playing. They help us by giving us messages of hope and joy when we most need it. They are the closest to our vibration so you may sense them before some of the higher vibrational Angels that have a higher frequency.

Archangels are such amazing helpers and I work with them all the time! Here is a list of some that you can call on and ask to assist you.

Please note: this list is just a sampling of the Archangels. I recommend finding books or classes that go into more detail on Angels and Archangels.

Michael: helps with protection, justice, and truth. Call on him for your safety with anything, especially things that feel energetically dark or heavy.

Raphael: Healing Angel of the Lord, known as the physician of the Angelic Realm, the Divine healer for healing ourselves and for helping to find the inner guidance, love, compassion, balance, and inspiration to heal others. He helps to develop Divine vision, intuition, and insight through balance and harmony. Enhances creative visualization and manifestation techniques. He is the Master Healer.

Gabriel: Helps with communication.

Uriel: One of the most powerful of the archangels and reflects the Divine light of God.

Metatron: Focus is spiritual evolution, enlightenment, light body activation, and ascension.

Jophiel: Focus is on wisdom. He brings soul illumination and strengthens the connection with the Higher Self, Guides, and Angels. His energy helps develop a fresh approach to life, bringing back enchantment, pleasure, and joy. He has a yellow flame of wisdom, intuition, bliss, and soul illumination.

Raziel: He helps to develop latent psychic abilities and aids conscious connection to Spirit. Raziel is the Archangel of the Secret Mysteries. He gives Divine information by allowing us to glimpse the enigma that is God. This takes us through consciousness through time and shows the past, present, and future as the eternal now. Sedates the conscious mind, which acts as a tranquilizer for emotions.

Zadkiel: Element of cosmic energy, balance expressed as cosmic consciousness, cosmic awareness, discernment, and understanding. He is the Angel of Mercy or Benevolence. Known as the holy one who teaches trust in God and the benevolence of God.

To connect with your angels, you need to elevate your vibration. My Spirit Guides have shown me that our vibrational ladder goes to a higher energetic dimension to reach the Angels. This is a higher dimension than you will need to go to than meeting your Spirit Guides.

Important note: when meeting your Angels in your sacred heart space, they can visit you there if your vibration is high enough. If you are spiritually traveling through dimensions (spirit journeying), then you will need to go to a higher plane to reach the Angels. There are many different dimensions of Angels.

I learned this when I began doing mediumship work. I was taught to rise right up to the highest possible vibration to meet with the Angels. I noticed that I had a hard time connecting to human spirits in the ultimate high vibrational plane. You can ask your guides to assist you in "climbing" your spiritual ladder of consciousness to meet your Guides, then you can raise higher to meet your Angels.

For me, this is the way I rode up and down the levels of consciousness while staying aware of my physical body. This is how I can channel this book and be in the 3D world at the same time.

I am raising my vibration as much as possible to be able to meet the Angels. They can shift or lower their vibration to meet with us somewhere in the middle.

If you aren't able to rise enough to be able to receive messages from your Angels, it could be because you have spiritual blocks that don't allow you to connect with them so clearly. I noticed this when I was at the beginning stages of awakening and was learning to connect with crystals. I remember picking up very high vibrational stones and having a high-pitched ringing in my ears that would calm down when I put the crystal back down. The ringing was very strong with a crystal called Danburite. I also noticed a huge shift when I bought Lapis Lazuli and had it sitting next to me in my bedroom. My husband was very affected by Lapis as well and he told me that he had very intense and amazing dreams after I brought it into the room. The crystals were helping me to bridge the gap in vibration between me and them.

Some crystals help strengthen your connection to the Angels.

Selenite, Kyanite, Apophyllite, Seraphinite, Amethyst, Smoky Quartz, Rose Quartz, Emerald, Celestite, Angelite, Moldavite, Black Tourmaline, Blue Lace Agate, and Green Prehnite are all crystals that help strengthen the connection to the Angels. I had amazing energetic responses with Danburite, which is a very vibrational stone. Please note that some of these crystals may feel too intense for you. In fact, I have seen people wear crystals that were too strong in energy for them. Moldavite is one of the highest vibrationally that I have felt. It is a meteorite and a form of tektite. I had a dear friend that was feeling out of sorts, and spacy. I noticed that she was wearing more than one large piece of Moldavite. I let her know that I felt that was what was affecting her. She took it off and stopped feeling the symptoms.

Moldavite is an amazing crystal, but it is so strong energetically that it can be too much, and I have had the same thing with other crystals. Do your research and make sure the crystals you wear are the right vibration for you. Rose quartz is a very soft and loving energy and is usually good for anyone. I recommend that you purchase a book on crystals so you can learn and be well-informed about them.

Another crystal that drew me was Seraphinite. It's named after Seraphim, the highest order of the angels, because of the feather-like markings on the stone. I can physically feel the energy and vibration from crystals, and this was another crystal that helps me feel the energy from the Angels. When I wear this crystal on a necklace, I feel like I'm on cloud nine!

As I did my inner work clearing out my shadows, each step moved me forward and upward into a higher level of consciousness. THIS is when I really began to feel and sense the energies of the Angels that were lovingly surrounding me. When I began doing energy healings and readings, I would psychically see or sense my client's Angels with them.

It is fascinating to see how Angels show themselves to me. Some look as large as a 5-story building, with wings that look like the drawings I've seen all my life. Most of the time I see them as beings of light and can change their shape into beautiful and different variations of light. The energy healing Angels turn into ribbons of colored light and float through my client's energy body. They help clean out the clutter and bring in the Divine and blissful ribbons of energy that you need to ascend. This helps to activate the dormant energetic DNA strands of your energy body.

Angels never mean harm and are trying to help you heal or give you direction. Many people are frightened of Angels because they don't understand them or have preconceived ideas of what they are. You should NOT have anything negative that approaches you when you work in the higher dimensions. Your Angels are simply trying to help you shed your own inner 'demons' that lie within your human self. Simply put, your Angels are here to help you slay your inner demons, which are emotionally angry parts of yourself that need healing. We all have emotional work to do, and they are patiently waiting for you to be ready to heal yourself.

~~~

Exercise

You can psychically fine-tune your ears (which are chakras) to hear your Angels and spirit guides. This is how!

You can do this by envisioning your ears and what the psychic antennae may look like that come from your ears and crown chakra. You may ask your Divine team of light, and especially your Angels, to help you do this.

Ground and clear your energy field. Call your team of light to help.

Take a deep breath and envision all your chakras spinning clockwise in your body, the energy running easily in your energy field, especially your crown, ears, and root chakras. This is cleansing your light body so you can be ready to work!

Envision funnel-shaped antennae made up of light that opens from your ears and crown and expands outward from your body. The funnels of energy open and have fine hairlike beams of light that go out from each ear and into the heavens and out the sides of your body. Envision this looking like a tuner for a radio that you can turn or change the station. Ask your Angels to assist you in "tuning" your stations to their frequency. Use your breath to move energy and feel the funnels of light (chakras) turning back and forth until they are on the correct channel or frequency to connect with your Divine spiritual team. Focus on the ears, and then focus on the crown chakra in the same way. Wearing or holding crystals that tap into Angel frequencies will also help. You will feel the funnels (chakras) spinning clockwise when they are running well. This is like an engine humming and connecting you to your Angels and guides!

Thank your Angels and know that you are "plugged in" to their frequency.

You may feel or sense more of these channels that have been disconnected, bent, or disfigured by energy. This may be due to harsh experiences, emotions, or by the changing of the Earth's rotation, magnetism, solar flares, and natural occurrences with the changing of time on Earth. Simply use your conscious thought and rebuild the antennae systems to the Divine!

You also have an antenna that goes down from your root chakra into Mother Earth. You can work on connecting that in when you ground your energy and ask her to help you "tune in" to her frequencies as well.

This is why I teach people to ground into the Earth, but also into the four directions. It helps you to stay balanced.

Please don't forget to thank your Angels! They have been there your whole life, trying to assist, and many times, being shunned and feared by humans! Ask them to come to you and invite them to help you daily. Let them know they are welcome in your life and when you send them gratitude, you reciprocate the loving energy between you both.

Chapter 16

Natural
VS
Learned
Mediumship

Chapter 16

Natural Mediumship vs Learned Mediumship, Working with Higher Self or Directly

When I discovered I was a medium, it was a shocking but welcomed experience. It was 2014, and my mother, Pat, had just recently passed away. I was speaking at her funeral and had jokingly asked her to come back and let me know the mysteries of the Universe such as ghost phenomena and Bigfoot. My mother was very intrigued with the supernatural and had some books from Sylvia Browne and other psychics that we both had read, which is why I joked about this. We watched ghost hunter shows and shows about great mysteries.

Little did I know that she was very much listening and had an agenda to help me on my path of spiritual awakening. While running outside on a road by my home right after she'd passed, I heard her shout at me that she was proud of me. It was her voice. I heard her loud and clear. Before that experience, and after, she came to me many times in dreams. I didn't remember anything we had discussed after waking, but I knew she was giving me very important information, along with letting me know that she was very happy and still with me. For the next few years, I read books written by famous mediums, but they didn't give me what I needed to understand how it worked. They didn't tell me how to do it myself.

My mother eventually got a very serious message through to me while chatting with me in my dreams one night. It was fascinating how she did this. I remembered her coming into my dreams and talking to me numerous times. I was very frustrated that I couldn't remember the conversations. She knew this, so the next time, she gave me the warning that my father, Fred, was having a serious problem with his memory, and that I would need to do something very soon to help him. After she told me, she pushed me backward, so I felt like I was falling backward, and I jerked awake. She did it! I was so excited! I remembered what she told me! It wasn't the best news, but I remembered! Of course, I then had to change course and take better care of my father, but that was ok!

Family members and spirit helpers come into our dreams to teach us things, and sometimes just to catch up and give us vital information that helps us on our life's path. My mother gave me important information that was critical to helping my father. At that time, he lived on his own, so no one could see how truly forgetful he had become. This knowledge helped us take better care of him before he hurt himself or someone else driving.

My father passed in 2016, and I was one of his caregivers at the time. While he was in hospice, I was able to see through the spiritual veils and dimensions. I slept in my living room with him the night before he passed. I was able to see him going back and forth from this physical plane to the Heavenly realm, visiting with my mother and his parents. After my father passed over, he also came and spoke to me. He always had a fascination with the first tribes of people in America and was very upset about how they were treated. He always said he "just knew" that he had been Native American in a past life. Two days after he passed, I asked him to come back to me and let me know which tribe he was from. He nodded and winked at me in agreement.

That was when I had the experience. It was within a week of his passing, and I sat on my couch scrolling on my phone on Facebook. I had a group that kept coming up that said I may be interested. I thought that was odd that it just came up out of the blue like that. I had a fleeting thought about this tribe, which was Cherokee. The word "Cherokee" floated into my mind. I brushed it off thinking, *Ok I don't believe that*. It felt like it was my own thought. The next night, I was sitting on the couch, scrolling again. This time I could smell my father and feel him standing on my left side. I could even feel his breath on my ear, and I heard him say, in his voice, *"I was Cherokee."* I got total body chills, and I didn't skip a beat this time. I knew that was dad. I said thanks to him for coming back and letting me know the answer from the other side.

These were experiences that just happened naturally to me. I can hear Spirit speaking to me, which means I am clairaudient. Spirit can speak directly to me, and I can hear them or hear the thoughts that they send to me.

I now set boundaries with my Spiritual Guides, especially my Gatekeeper, so that I am safe. I set boundaries when I allow spirits to talk to me, and if they haven't crossed over, then only under certain circumstances if they are negative or angry humans.

You can choose whatever you'd like and find what fits you if you are a natural medium. You may also choose for messages to only come through your Higher Self. If you feel uncomfortable with spirits talking directly to you, then you can ask your Higher Self to come and be a mediator to bring you the information you need from people in spirit.

What makes you comfortable? If you have any fears, or worries about doing this work, then ask your Higher Self to assist.

Ask them to discern what would be comfortable for you. After all, they are you, but in a higher vibration and with many more tricks up their sleeves. They know your fears, your worries and can put your mind at ease when doing this work.

If you haven't had any experiences yet with mediumship, then you will need to do the work to help you open spiritually to be able to have those connections and experiences with people in spirit. Meditation is the key. Meditation, spirit journeys, and inner soul work are the keys to helping you open to connect with the World of Spirit. Trust in yourself! If you feel frustrated, then quit and try again later. Keep your spirits lifted and happy as much as possible. If you find the door is shut for you, then pivot and try another way, such as tarot, oracle, or Angel cards.

Not everyone will be a master medium! We all have spiritual abilities that are different from each other. You may not be a natural at mediumship, but you may be amazing at something else! Allow yourself to explore different avenues within the psychic world. I have mentioned many that you can explore! The more you PLAY, the more you will grow spiritually. This is why it can be so much fun! This isn't work, it is fun! If you see it that way, then you won't put so much pressure on yourself to be perfect.

If you can find a way to get some kind of message from your Divine helpers, then you are moving forward! Appreciate even the smallest of accomplishments! Have a small private party every time you get a "hit" of information that is accurate. Don't give up.

~~~

Exercise

Opening and Closing a Reading Session for Someone

Opening a session/reading:

If you are doing a psychic or mediumship reading for someone else, it is important to set your intentions, clear your space and call in your high vibrational team of light. You may feel like a special prayer, mantra or intention is a good way for you to begin your readings as well. You may choose to make up your own or use a prayer you have from someone else that resonates with you. I suggest going within and doing a meditation where you focus on what that prayer would consist of.

I ask that all my Divine helpers of light come in and assist me, give me clear and Divine guidance. I also ask that they help me stay safe while giving messages to others that help them be uplifted. Whatever you choose to begin the reading, this is much like opening a door to their soul, and therefore, is setting the intentions for you and them at the same time.

Closing session/reading:

When you are finished with the reading and have no more messages for your client, you will need to envision closing that door that connects your soul to theirs. When you open that door, you are interconnecting to their auric field, and receiving messages while in their personal energetic space. You are also tapping into a Divine radio frequency that connects to you and them at the same time. This is how your heavenly helpers give you the information you need to relay to your client.

In your mind's eye, envision stepping back from them and clapping your hands or brushing them together to disconnect from their energy field. You can also do this physically if you feel it is necessary. Whether you envision closing the door or clapping your hands, you are setting the intention that you are disconnecting from their energy field, which is very important. After all, you don't want to be interconnected with that person's inner secrets and energy after you have completed the reading.

When the person has left, do a cleansing of your energy field by calling in your spiritual team to energetically vacuum your light body of any energies that you may have retained from your client. This can be emotional or energetic baggage or energetic connections (cords) to them. **It is very important that you clear this energy from yourself.** Ask your Angels to help you pull out anything that is not your energy and pull it out into a wall of Angelic light. Take a deep breath in, and on the breath out, envision anything that is not your energy leaving your body and going into that wall of Angelic light, and then back to your client.

Then call your energy back from them through that wall of Divine light and back to you. Feel it fill your entire body, filling you with immense light and joy.

You can also create a room of light that is like a car wash but is made of multi-colored light energies that flow through your body and cleanse and clear you. You have many options on how to clear your energy. I love to create a space where you go through a vacuum-sealed room and when you walk through it you are sparkling clean. You can imagine you are walking into a rainbow sparkling waterfall and it is clearing you from head to toe.

Important note: Do not forget to send the Divine energy through your whole light body around you, your entire auric field. That is part of your energy as well and can hold energies from experiences and thoughts that aren't pleasant.

Ground your energy in all four directions, call your energy back to the heart space, and open your eyes.

Important personal note: I ask my Guides and Angels to help me to do this disconnection and clearing of my client's energy even if I forget. This is very important to me because I had the experience after doing a reading where I woke up with negative dreams one night, which was unusual for me at that period of my life. I immediately asked my guides what these terrible dreams were about, and they told me that I didn't clear my energy from the client from that day. I was still tapped into her energy, and it wasn't pleasant. I immediately cleared from her energy, and I haven't forgotten since! And even if I do forget to do this very important step, I know my guides and Angels step up and let me know or do it for me.

Chapter 17

You are a beacon of light!

Chapter 17

You Are Now on Your Way! You Are a Beacon of Light! How Do You Want to Proceed?

It is such an honor to share my experiences with all of you. I'm not going to lie, there have been many times that I wanted to give up because this work is sometimes grueling and hard to go through. There have been times that I felt my Guides let me down and I got mad at them for guiding me in a situation that was hard to deal with. I remember a few times being very angry and letting them know I was pissed! The thing is, they guided me into experiences that made me grow as a soul and soar into a new experience that was more on the path I wanted to be on. I didn't come here to experience this life to play it safe, I came here to experience the rawness and grit, to learn to find my way, and to help make the world a better place. I came here to shine, and that meant I had to make many changes in ME for me to do so.

I say this all the time – I am so happy to be able to. I am now doing what I came here on Earth to do. I am living my true purpose. I am doing work that helps me feel fulfilled by assisting others to achieve this same way of living. I wake up happy to do my spiritual work every day. I have made a conscious effort to move out of jobs and experiences that made me miserable. I made a conscious effort after learning about the law of attraction to better my life in little ways each day until I no longer felt angry, sick, and victimized in life. I am no longer living in the rat race, unaware of who I really AM!

If you aren't living each day in joy, make changes to live your life each day to live in joy, happiness, and peace. Let go of things that frustrate you and make you unhappy. If you can learn to fill your cup, it will overflow so that you may give to others of your own free will. Allow those who no longer resonate with you to fall away. As you raise your vibration, you will have friends and family that no longer connect with you. You may change, and they may not, or it may be the opposite. This can be a heartbreaking part of this experience, but as you shift, you move on and move forward. This can feel lonely. Like no one understands you. I am here to tell you, many understand you. You are not alone! You are learning to live a life of truth and substance. You find that lies or untruths are suddenly not a possibility for you. You speak your truth; you can't handle small talk that has no meaning. You want to talk about the universe, the stars, and love. You may feel like walking away when you are with someone who is bad-mouthing others or gossiping. Allow yourself to move on from those old experiences so you can blossom, and you will be drawn to others like yourself that are ready for a new type of existence, and a new life!

We choose how we treat each other, and now, for me, I choose to respect others, and I choose to be respected. That took many years of self-worth work. I now know I deserve this respect when previously, I never even thought about it. We are all just at different parts of our respective life journeys.

How do you choose to live your life? For me, I am spiritual but not quiet. In the past, I believed that to be spiritual, you had to be quiet, and sit and meditate for days on end.

NOT ME.

I love to dance and hang out with friends. I love to ride roller coasters and scream my lungs out having fun. I love to go to rock concerts, go on camping adventures, and hike through the mountains with my sister, Cindy. I love my daughters and their husbands, and most of all, I love my dear husband, Tim, who has always been my rock. My spiritual awakening affected him. As a matter of fact, he was much more spiritually awake than I was for many years. My dark night of the soul began when I got injured by a softball in 2010. I had a traumatic injury with a softball to the face that crushed my right eye socket and split my face. That is what started me on the journey of looking at all my darkness, followed by my parents' deaths, and then my spiritual rebirth when doing all my inner spiritual work!

My Spirit Guides tell me my stubbornness was the reason I had to be physically whacked by a ball. We call this being hit by a cosmic two-by-four. I laugh because I know they are right! That started me on the path of really seeing what was behind the curtain! There is the most gorgeous Divine light that is beyond that curtain.

In my dreams, after my mother's death, she came to me and showed me a beautiful theatre with a big stage that had a velvety indigo-colored curtain. She pulled it back and showed me the light of Source that shined into me. I could feel the Divine light pour into me.

A few months after that, in meditation, she appeared again, but this time she tore down the whole curtain. I felt like I lit up from inside my heart, shining rays of sunshine in every direction from my heart.

Many veils for each of us act like walls that block us from our true Divine essence, and Source.

I hope this book helps you to tear down your curtains and veils that are just smoky illusions that keep you from knowing who you are.

You are a Divine being of love consciousness. Shine your light for all to see. Live your life for joy, and I will do the same.

I see you.

It is an honor to be your living guide.

Much love and well wishes on your most magical journey of all!

Kathleen

Bibliography

"Psychic Definition & Meaning." Merriam-Webster. Merriam-Webster. Accessed February 25, 2023. https://www.merriam-webster.com/dictionary/psychic.

"Mediumship Definition & Meaning." Merriam-Webster. Merriam-Webster. Accessed February 25, 2023. https://www.merriam-webster.com/dictionary/mediumship.

"Divination Definition & Meaning." Merriam-Webster. Merriam-Webster. Accessed February 25, 2023. https://www.merriam-webster.com/dictionary/divination.

"Telekinesis Definition & Meaning." Merriam-Webster. Merriam-Webster. Accessed February 25, 2023. https://www.merriam-webster.com/dictionary/telekinesis.

"Psychometry Definition & Meaning." Merriam-Webster. Merriam-Webster. Accessed February 25, 2023. https://www.merriam-webster.com/dictionary/psychometry.

"List of Psychic Abilities." Wikipedia. Wikimedia Foundation, February 24, 2023. https://en.wikipedia.org/wiki/List_of_psychic_abilities.

"Angel Definition & Meaning." Merriam-Webster. Merriam-Webster. Accessed February 25, 2023. https://www.merriam-webster.com/dictionary/angel.

Raven, Hazel. The Angel Bible: The Definitive Guide to Angel Wisdom. London: Godsfield, 2009.

"De Coelesti Hierarchia." Wikipedia. Wikimedia Foundation, January 16, 2023. https://en.wikipedia.org/wiki/De_Coelesti_Hierarchia.

About The Author

Kathleen Sherman
Quantum Shamanic Intuitive LLC

Kathleen Sherman is a natural shaman, medical intuitive, psychic medium, Angel channel, Reiki master, spiritual mentor, and author.

Kathleen combines medical intuition, shamanism, and quantum healing to help her clients in all stages of the ascension process. In addition, she can view past lives and channels loving spirit guides and Angels to help guide clients to heal body, mind, and spirit.

Kathleen's Certifications include:

*Medical Intuition and Advanced Medical Intuition Certification.

*Certified Professional Master Life Coach including Life Purpose, Happiness, and Shamanic Life Coach Certifications

*Certified Master Hypnotherapist and Hypnotist

*Certified Past Life Regressionist

*Certified Reiki Master-Usui Reiki Ryoho

Go to **KathleenShermanHealing.net** to book a session, take an online class, or purchase one or both of her books!

Kathleen Sherman

Medical Intuitive | Kathleen Sherman

Are you seeking profound transformation, holistic healing, and spiritual guidance? Look no further. Kathleen Sherman is your trusted Shamanic Medical Intuitive, Psychic Medium, Reiki Master, and Quantum Energy Healer. With a wealth of experience and a deep connection to the unseen realms, Kathleen is here to guide you on your journey to wellness and enlightenment.

KathleenShermanHealing.net
SCAN TO VISIT WEBSITE

Kathleen Sherman
Quantum Shamanic Intuitive LLC

About The Editor

With a love for words and languages, Angela Haworth took her passion from writing to editing with JOTZY Creatives. As a published author and editor, she provides the keen eye, creativity, and knowledge to ensure her client's readers are engaged, captured, enthralled, and left wanting more.

As Kathleen's editor, I have had the most enjoyable experience working with her. This guidebook, along with her first, is her gift to those who are willing and ready to awaken to their true soul's purpose. My gift to you is to help her communicate clearly to you how to do this. I am excited about Kathleen's next channeled book as I know it will hold many more keys on how to open to your life's purpose.

For editorial support, you can contact Angela:

Website: https://www.jotzycreatives.com/

Facebook: https://www.facebook.com/JOTZYCreatives

email: JOTZYCreatives@gmail.com

Made in the USA
Monee, IL
23 September 2023